HARCOURT

Math

Harcourt School Publishers
Orlando • Boston • Dallas • Chicago • San Diego
www.harcourtschool.com

For permission to reprint copyrighted material, grateful acknowledgment is made to the following sources:

Aladdin Paperbacks, an imprint of Simon & Schuster Children's Publishing Division: Cover illustration by Ron Barrett from *Benjamin's 365 Birthdays* by Judi Barrett. Illustration copyright © 1974 by Ron Barrett. Cover illustration by Nancy Winslow Parker from *The Goat in the Rug* as told to Charles L. Blood & Martin Link by Geraldine. Illustration copyright © 1976 by Nancy Winslow Parker. Cover illustration by Ray Cruz from *Alexander, Who Used to be Rich Last Sunday* by Judith Viorst. Illustration copyright © 1978 by Ray Cruz.

Dial Books for Young Readers, a division of Penguin Putnam Inc.: Cover illustration by Devis Grebu from *The King's Chessboard* by David Birch. Illustration copyright © 1988 by Devis Grebu. Cover illustration by Patricia MacCarthy from *17 Kings and 42 Elephants* by Margaret Mahy. Illustration copyright © 1987 by Patricia MacCarthy.

Four Winds Press: Cover illustration by Cyndy Szekeres from *The 329th Friend* by Marjorie Weinman Sharmat. Illustration copyright © 1979 by Cyndy Szekeres.

Greenwillow Books, a division of William Morrow & Company, Inc.: Cover illustration by Donald Crews from *Each Orange Had 8 Slices: A Counting Book* by Paul Giganti, Jr. Illustration copyright © 1992 by Donald Crews. Cover illustration by Donald Crews from *How Many Snails? a Counting Book* by Paul Giganti, Jr. Illustration copyright © 1988 by Donald Crews.

Harcourt, Inc.: Cover illustration from *The Twelve Circus Rings* by Seymour Chwast. Copyright © 1993 by Seymour Chwast. Cover illustration from *How Big Were the Dinosaurs?* by Bernard Most. Copyright © 1994 by Bernard Most.

HarperCollins Publishers: Cover illustration from *Arthur's Funny Money* by Lillian Hoban. Copyright © 1981 by Lillian Hoban. Cover illustration by S. D. Schindler from *BETCHA!* by Stuart J. Murphy. Illustration copyright © 1997 by S. D. Schindler. Cover illustration by George Ulrich from *Divide and Ride* by Stuart J. Murphy. Illustration copyright © 1997 by George Ulrich. Cover illustration by John Speirs from *A Fair Bear Share* by Stuart J. Murphy. Illustration copyright © 1998 by The Big Cheese Design, Inc. Cover illustration by Steven Kellogg from *If You Made a Million* by David M. Schwartz. Illustration copyright © 1989 by Steven Kellogg. Cover illustration by Jon Buller from *Ready, Set, Hop!* by Stuart J. Murphy. Illustration copyright © 1996 by Jon Buller.

Henry Holt and Company, LLC: Cover illustration from *The Empty Pot* by Demi. Copyright © 1990 by Demi. Cover illustration from *Measuring Penny* by Loreen Leedy. Copyright © 1997 by Loreen Leedy.

Houghton Mifflin Company: Cover illustration by Bonnie MacKain from *One Hundred Hungry Ants* by Elinor J. Pinczes. Illustration copyright © 1993 by Bonnie MacKain.

Hyperion Books for Children: Cover illustration by Carol Schwartz from *Sea Sums* by Joy N. Hulme. Illustration © 1996 by Carol Schwartz.

Little, Brown and Company Inc.: Cover illustration from *The Village of Round and Square Houses* by Ann Grifalconi. Copyright © 1986 by Ann Grifalconi.

North-South Books Inc., New York: Cover illustration from *A Birthday Cake for Little Bear* by Max Velthuijs, translated by Rosemary Lanning. Copyright © 1988 by Nord-Süd Verlag AG, Gossau Zurich, Switzerland.

Philomel Books, a division of Penguin Putnam Inc.: Cover illustration from *Anno's Math Games II* by Mitsumasa Anno. Copyright © 1982 by Kuso Kobo; translation and special contents of this edition copyright © 1989 by Philomel Books. Cover illustration by Mitsumasa Anno from *Anno's Mysterious Multiplying Jar* by Masaichiro and Mitsumasa Anno. Text translation copyright © 1983 by Philomel Books; copyright © 1982 by Kuso Kobo.

Scholastic Inc.: Cover illustration by Susan Guevara from *The King's Commissioners* by Aileen Friedman. A Marilyn Burns Brainy Day Book. Copyright © 1994 by Marilyn Burns Education Associates. Published by Scholastic Press, a division of Scholastic Inc. Cover photograph from *Eating Fractions* by Bruce McMillan. Copyright © 1991 by Bruce McMillan. SCHOLASTIC HARDCOVER is a registered trademark of Scholastic Inc.

Simon & Schuster Books for Young Readers, an imprint of Simon & Schuster Children's Publishing Division: Cover illustration from *Clocks and More Clocks* by Pat Hutchins. Copyright © 1970 by Pat Hutchins. Cover illustration by Sharon McGinley-Nally from *Pigs Will Be Pigs* by Amy Axelrod. Illustration copyright © 1994 by Sharon McGinley-Nally.

Viking Penguin, a division of Penguin Putnam Inc.: Cover illustration by Leo and Diane Dillon: from *The Hundred Penny Box* by Sharon Bell Mathis. Illustration copyright © 1975 by Leo and Diane Dillon.

Albert Whitman & Company: Cover illustration from *Two of Everything* by Lily Toy Hong. © 1993 by Lily Toy Hong.

Printed in the United States of America

ISBN 0-15-320746-9 (Grade Level Book)

ISBN 0-15-322051-1 (Unit Book Collection)

16 17 18 19 20 21 030 2013 2012 2011 2010 2009

Senior Author

Evan M. Maletsky
Professor of Mathematics
Montclair State University
Upper Montclair, New Jersey

Mathematics Advisor

David G. Wright
Professor of Mathematics
Brigham Young University
Provo, Utah

Authors

Angela Giglio Andrews
Math Teacher, Scott School
Naperville District #203
Naperville, Illinois

Jennie M. Bennett
Instructional Mathematics Supervisor
Houston Independent School District
Houston, Texas

Grace M. Burton
Chair, Department of Curricular Studies
Professor, School of Education
University of North Carolina at Wilmington
Wilmington, North Carolina

Howard C. Johnson
Dean of the Graduate School
Associate Vice Chancellor for Academic Affairs
Professor, Mathematics and Mathematics Education
Syracuse University
Syracuse, New York

Lynda A. Luckie
Administrator/Math Specialist
Gwinnett County Public Schools
Lawrenceville, Georgia

Joyce C. McLeod
Visiting Professor
Rollins College
Winter Park, Florida

Vicki Newman
Classroom Teacher
McGaugh Elementary School
Los Alamitos Unified School District
Seal Beach, California

Janet K. Scheer
Executive Director
Create A Vision
Foster City, California

Karen A. Schultz
College of Education
Georgia State University
Atlanta, Georgia

Program Consultants and Specialists

Janet S. Abbott
Mathematics Consultant
California

Elsie Babcock
Director, Mathematics and Science Center
Mathematics Consultant
Wayne Regional Educational Service Agency
Wayne, Michigan

William J. Driscoll
Professor of Mathematics
Department of Mathematical Sciences
Central Connecticut State University
New Britain, Connecticut

Lois Harrison-Jones
Education and Management Consultant
Dallas, Texas

Arax Miller
Curriculum Coordinator and English Department Chairperson
Chamlian School
Glendale, California

Rebecca Valbuena
Language Development Specialist
Stanton Elementary School
Glendora, California

NUMBERS, OPERATIONS, AND DATA

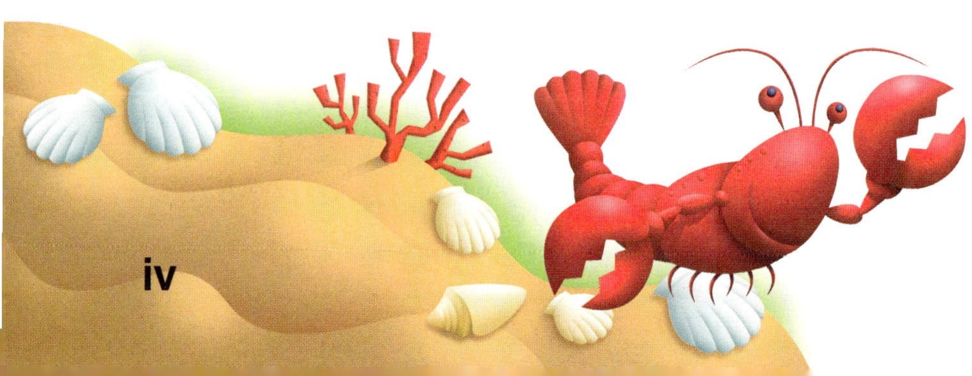

Unit Wrap Up

MONEY AND TIME

7 COUNTING MONEY

8 USING MONEY

Unit Wrap Up

2-DIGIT ADDITION AND SUBTRACTION

Unit Wrap Up

GEOMETRY AND MEASUREMENT

Unit Wrap Up

NUMBER SENSE AND FRACTIONS

Unit Wrap Up

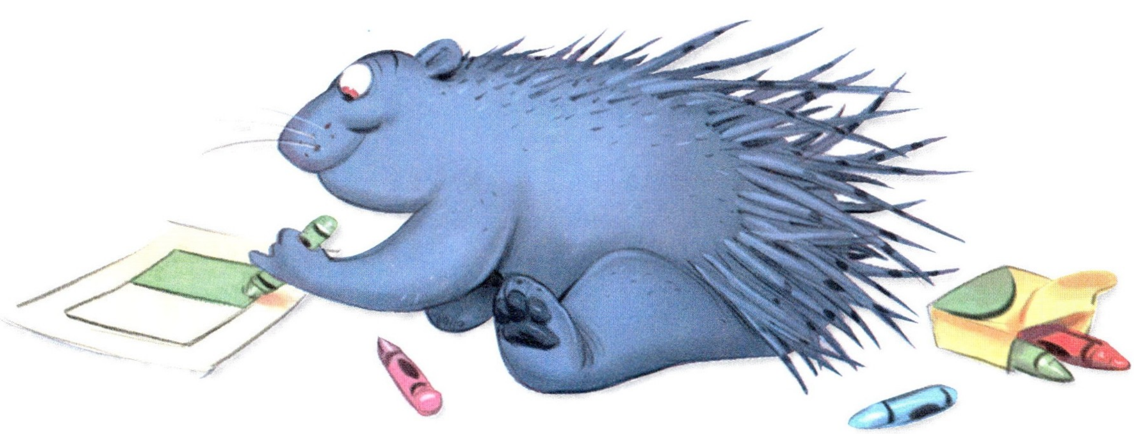

3-DIGIT ADDITION AND SUBTRACTION, MULTIPLICATION AND DIVISION

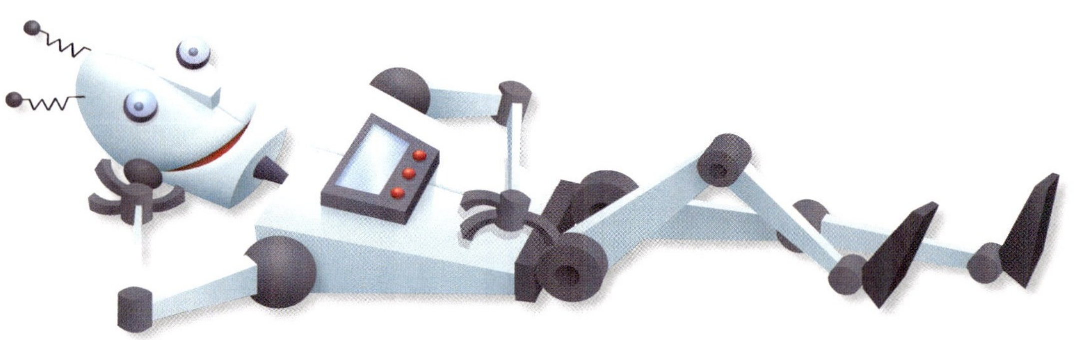

Unit Wrap Up

SCHOOL HOME CONNECTION

Dear Family,

Today we started our math book. Before we begin Chapter 1, we will go over some of the things that we learned last year.

Here are a few important things to know about my new book. At the beginning of each chapter is a Home Letter that tells you the new vocabulary words, lists some books for us to share, and describes an activity we can do. Each lesson has a Home Activity so I can show you what I am learning. At the end of each unit there is a Math Storybook that will help me show you what I have learned.

Love,

____

Visit ***The Learning Site*** **for additional ideas and activities. www.harcourtschool.com**

Getting Ready for Grade 2

HOME ACTIVITY • In *Getting Ready*, your child will review ones and tens of the place value system, add and subtract basic facts, and measure and locate objects in space. Your child will describe data and solve simple problems.

Name ______________________________

Count by twos. Color each number.
Count by fives. Circle each number.

1

1	2	3	4	5	6	7	8	9	10
11	12	13	14	15	16	17	18	19	20
21	22	23	24	25	26	27	28	29	30
31	32	33	34	35	36	37	38	39	40
41	42	43	44	45	46	47	48	49	50

Circle the statements that are correct.

2

$83 > 81$	$46 = 40 + 6$	$5 = 50$
$59 > 95$	$75 > 45$	$32 > 31$

Name ______________________________

Write the number that tells how many.

1

______

2

______

Draw base ten blocks to show how many.

3

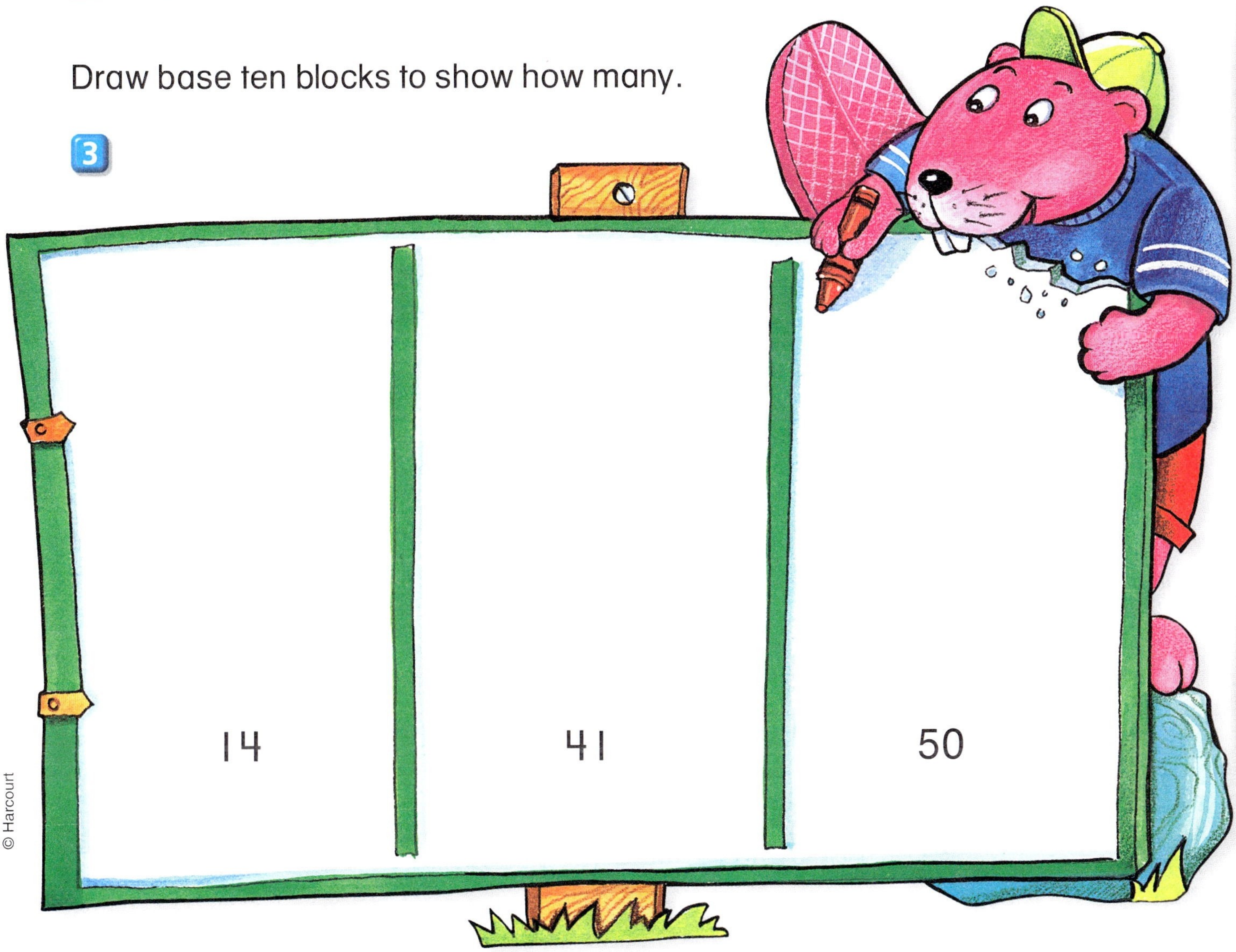

Name ______________________________

Add or subtract.

4 + 2 = ____	10 − 2 = ____	7 + 2 = ____
6 + 1 = ____	9 − 1 = ____	9 − 2 = ____
8 + 2 = ____	7 − 3 = ____	9 + 1 = ____
7 + 3 = ____	8 − 4 = ____	5 + 5 = ____
4 + 4 = ____	8 − 8 = ____	10 − 4 = ____
4 + 5 = ____	10 − 3 = ____	9 − 6 = ____
6 + 3 = ____	6 − 4 = ____	6 + 2 = ____
8 + 0 = ____	9 − 5 = ____	10 − 7 = ____

Name ______________________________

Use 🟡. Draw them.
Write the number sentence.

Three boys. Three girls.
How many children in all?

1

_____ ◯ _____ = _____ children

Write the number sentence.

There are 9 birds. 4 birds leave.
How many birds are left?

2

_____ ◯ _____ = _____ birds

Name ______________________________

About how long is the string? Use .

1

______ 

2

______ 

Use the chart.
Make a bar graph.

3

Favorite Colors	
red	卌 III
yellow	III
blue	卌 I

Favorite Colors										
red										
yellow										
blue										
	0	1	2	3	4	5	6	7	8	9	10

Name ______________________________

Follow the directions.

1. Draw a red square.

2. Draw a large green triangle above the red square.

3. Draw a small blue circle below the red square.

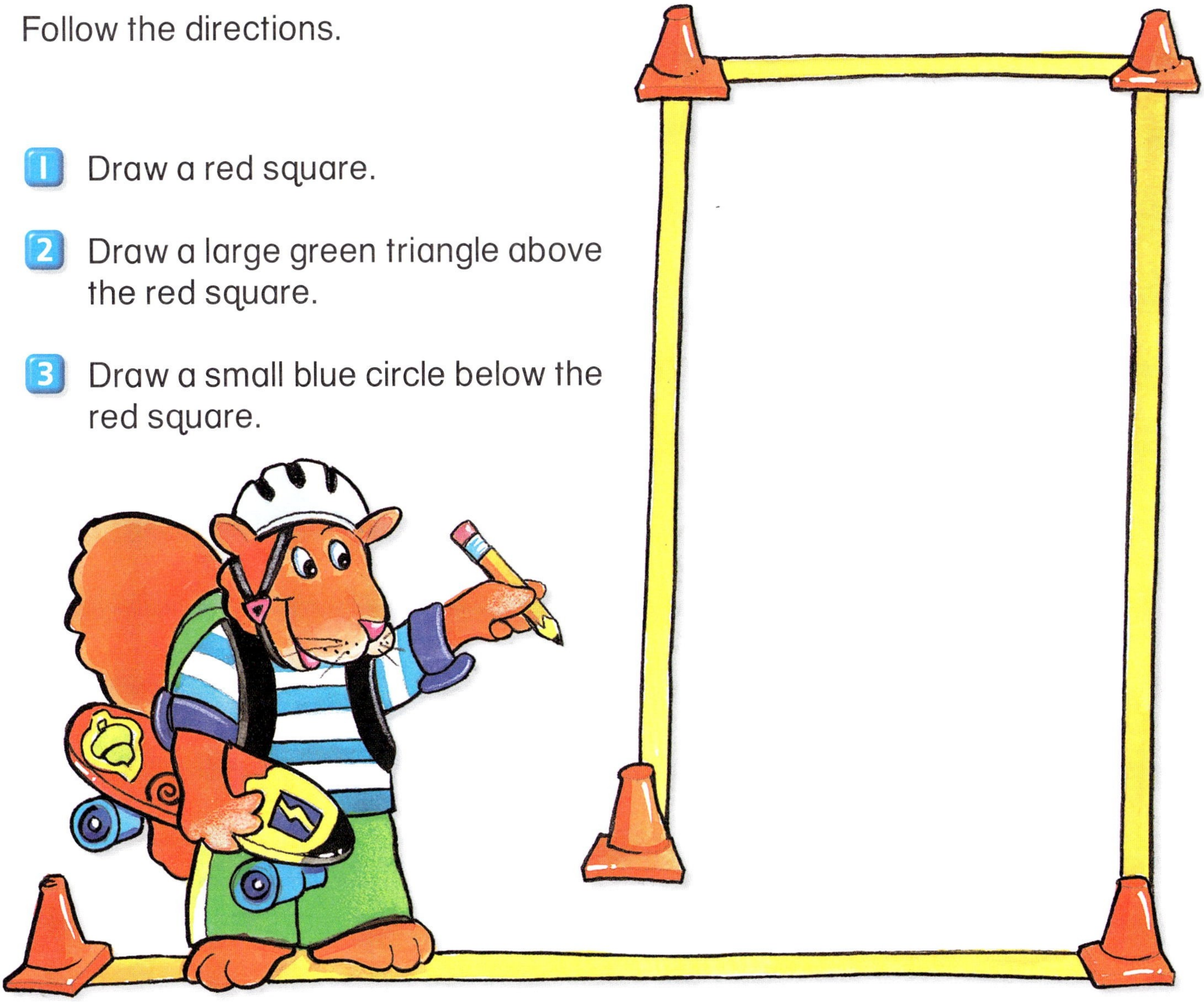

Use the same shapes to make a different pattern.
Draw your new pattern .

4.

Name ______________________________

Show a way to solve this problem.

I have some teddy bears. I gave 3 of them away. Now I have 7. How many teddy bears did I have to start?

I had ______ teddy bears to start.

Talk About It

How do you know that your answer makes sense?
Tell how you solved this problem.

CHAPTER 1 Addition Strategies

What addition sentences can you write about this picture?

School Home Connection

Dear Family,

Today we started Chapter 1. We will learn addition facts to 20. We will also learn addition strategies to help us solve problems. Here is the math vocabulary and an activity for us to do together at home.

Love,

____

My Math Words

doubles plus one

sum

Vocabulary

doubles plus one Addition facts whose sums are one more than the sum of a doubles fact

doubles

7 + 7 = 14

doubles plus one

7 + 8 = 15

sum The sum is the answer when numbers are added.

Visit *The Learning Site* for additional ideas and activities. www.harcourtschool.com

Activity

Fold a piece of paper into four sections, and write one of these problems in each section.

3 + 6 = ___	4 + 3 = ___
5 + 2 = ___	7 + 3 = ___

Have your child draw pictures to find each sum.

Books to Share

To read about addition with your child, look for these books in your local library.

Two of Everything, by Lily Toy Hong, Albert Whitman, 1993.

The Pig in the Pond, by Martin Waddell, Candlewick, 1996.

Name ______________________________

Order and Zero Properties

Algebra

Changing the **order** of the **addends** does not change the **sum**.

Any number plus **zero** **equals** the same number.

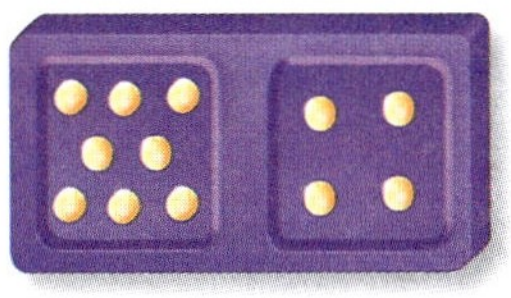

8 + 4 = 12

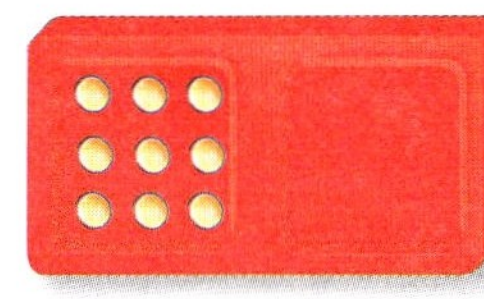

9 + 0 = 9

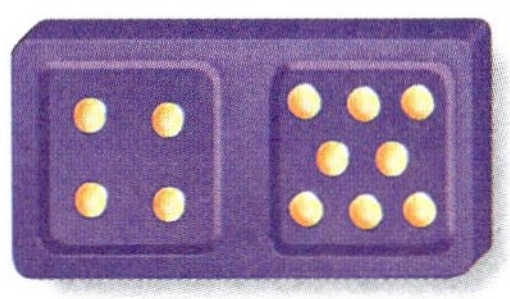

4 + 8 = 12

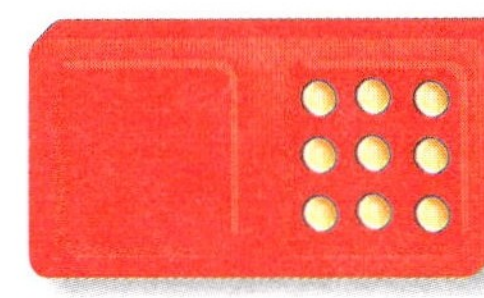

0 + 9 = 9

Write the sum.

1. 5 + 4 = 9
   4 + 5 = 9

2. 10 + 0 = ____
   0 + 10 = ____

3. 7 + 5 = ____
   5 + 7 = ____

4. 6 + 4 = ____
   4 + 6 = ____

5. 3 + 9 = ____
   9 + 3 = ____

6. 0 + 11 = ____
   11 + 0 = ____

7. 0 + 8 = ____
   8 + 0 = ____

8. 4 + 7 = ____
   7 + 4 = ____

9. 6 + 0 = ____
   0 + 6 = ____

Talk About It ■ Reasoning

What happens to the sum when you change the order of the addends?
What happens when you add a number to zero?

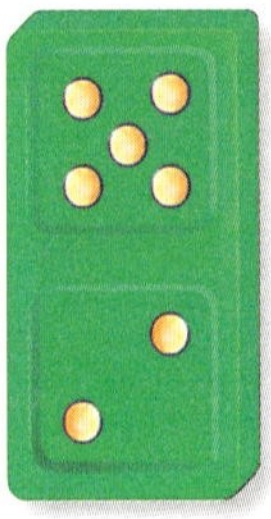 $\begin{array}{r}5\\+2\\\hline 7\end{array}$ 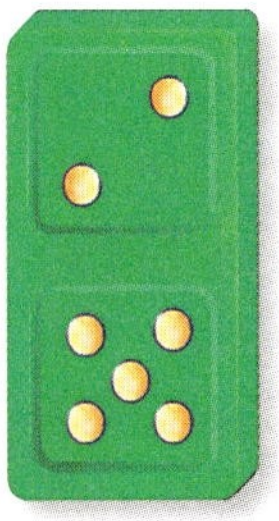 $\begin{array}{r}2\\+5\\\hline 7\end{array}$

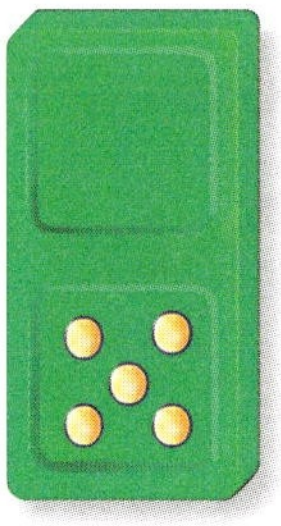 $\begin{array}{r}0\\+5\\\hline 5\end{array}$  $\begin{array}{r}5\\+0\\\hline 5\end{array}$

Write the sum.

1. $\begin{array}{r}3\\+2\\\hline\end{array}$ $\begin{array}{r}2\\+3\\\hline\end{array}$

2. $\begin{array}{r}12\\+0\\\hline\end{array}$ $\begin{array}{r}0\\+12\\\hline\end{array}$

3. $\begin{array}{r}4\\+1\\\hline\end{array}$ $\begin{array}{r}1\\+4\\\hline\end{array}$

4. $\begin{array}{r}6\\+3\\\hline\end{array}$ $\begin{array}{r}3\\+6\\\hline\end{array}$

5. $\begin{array}{r}8\\+2\\\hline\end{array}$ $\begin{array}{r}2\\+8\\\hline\end{array}$

6. $\begin{array}{r}6\\+5\\\hline\end{array}$ $\begin{array}{r}5\\+6\\\hline\end{array}$

Problem Solving ■ Visual Thinking

7. Color these cubes to show $3 + 6 = 9$.

Tell how you would change the colors to show $6 + 3 = 9$.

HOME ACTIVITY • Have your child use small objects to show an addition fact. Change the order of the addends, and have your child show the new fact.

Name ______________________________

Count On 1, 2, and 3

Start with the **greater** number. **Count on** to find the sum.

Say 8. Count on 1. **9** The sum is 9.	Say 8. Count on 2. **9, 10** The sum is 10.	Say 8. Count on 3. **9, 10, 11** The sum is 11.
$8 + 1 = 9$	$8 + 2 = 10$	$8 + 3 = 11$

Circle the greater number.
Count on to find the sum.

1	$9 + 1$	$9 + 2$	$9 + 3$	$2 + 7$	$8 + 2$	$3 + 9$
2	$7 + 1$	$2 + 7$	$7 + 3$	$1 + 8$	$2 + 9$	$2 + 10$
3	$10 + 3$	$8 + 3$	$2 + 6$	$8 + 1$	$2 + 8$	$3 + 8$

Talk About It ■ Reasoning

Why is it easier to start with the greater number when counting on?

3+9=12

Circle the greater number.
Count on to find the sum.

1 $3 + 9 =$ 12	2 $9 + 2 =$ ____	3 $1 + 9 =$ ____
4 $2 + 9 =$ ____	5 $7 + 2 =$ ____	6 $10 + 1 =$ ____
7 $1 + 4 =$ ____	8 $4 + 2 =$ ____	9 $3 + 4 =$ ____
10 $3 + 10 =$ ____	11 $1 + 8 =$ ____	12 $9 + 2 =$ ____
13 $6 + 2 =$ ____	14 $4 + 3 =$ ____	15 $2 + 8 =$ ____
16 $6 + 1 =$ ____	17 $2 + 5 =$ ____	18 $10 + 2 =$ ____

Problem Solving ■ Mental Math

Find the sum.

19 Rob has 7 shirts. Ed has 2 more than Rob. How many shirts does Ed have?

____ shirts

20 Susan has 3 pennies. Mary has 5 more than Susan. How many pennies does Mary have?

____ pennies

HOME ACTIVITY • Have your child tell an addition story for each picture in this lesson.

Name ______________________

Doubles and Doubles Plus One

doubles | **doubles plus one**

Write the sum. Write the doubles-plus-one fact.

1. $5 + 5 = \underline{10}$
   $\underline{5} + \underline{6} = \underline{11}$

2. $7 + 7 =$ ____
   ____ + ____ = ____

3. $6 + 6 =$ ____
   ____ + ____ = ____

4. $3 + 3 =$ ____
   ____ + ____ = ____

5. $8 + 8 =$ ____
   ____ + ____ = ____

6. $9 + 9 =$ ____
   ____ + ____ = ____

7. $4 + 4 =$ ____
   ____ + ____ = ____

8. $2 + 2 =$ ____
   ____ + ____ = ____

Talk About It ■ Reasoning

How does knowing a doubles fact help you know a doubles-plus-one fact?

Practice

Put a triangle in the doubles answer boxes. Then write the sum.
Put a square in the doubles-plus-one answer boxes. Then write the sum.
Complete the addition table.

+	0	1	2	3	4	5	6	7	8	9	10
0	△ 0	□			4	5	6				
1									9	10	
2	2			5		7					
3											
4		5	6				10		12	13	
5				8	9						
6	6	7	8								16
7			9		11						
8							14	15	16	17	
9			11	12							
10	10					15	16	17			

HOME ACTIVITY • Ask your child how knowing the sum of 3 + 3 helps him or her know the sum of 3 + 4.

Name ______________________

Make a Ten

Add 8 + 5.

Use a ten frame.
Put in 8 counters.
Put 5 counters outside.

$$\begin{array}{r} 8 \\ +5 \\ \hline \end{array}$$

Then **make a ten**.
Move 2 counters
to fill the ten frame.
8 + 2 = 10

Add 10 and 3.
10 + 3 = 13

$$\begin{array}{r} 10 \\ +\ 3 \\ \hline 13 \end{array}$$

Use a ten frame and 🟡 to make a ten.
Find the sum.

1	8 + 5 = 13	7 + 6	6 + 9	4 + 6	8 + 4	8 + 6
2	3 + 7	9 + 2	7 + 7	4 + 8	5 + 7	9 + 8
3	8 + 7	9 + 4	5 + 9	6 + 6	4 + 7	8 + 3

Talk About It ■ **Reasoning**

When you set up an addition problem, why do you put the greater number in the ten frame?

Use a ten frame and ● to find the sum.

$$\begin{array}{r} 5 \\ +8 \\ \hline ? \end{array}$$

1

$\begin{array}{r} 5 \\ +8 \\ \hline 13 \end{array}$	$\begin{array}{r} 8 \\ +6 \\ \hline \end{array}$	$\begin{array}{r} 9 \\ +6 \\ \hline \end{array}$	$\begin{array}{r} 5 \\ +9 \\ \hline \end{array}$	$\begin{array}{r} 9 \\ +8 \\ \hline \end{array}$	$\begin{array}{r} 8 \\ +7 \\ \hline \end{array}$

2

$\begin{array}{r} 9 \\ +2 \\ \hline \end{array}$	$\begin{array}{r} 8 \\ +4 \\ \hline \end{array}$	$\begin{array}{r} 9 \\ +7 \\ \hline \end{array}$	$\begin{array}{r} 7 \\ +7 \\ \hline \end{array}$	$\begin{array}{r} 3 \\ +8 \\ \hline \end{array}$	$\begin{array}{r} 7 \\ +6 \\ \hline \end{array}$

3

$\begin{array}{r} 5 \\ +7 \\ \hline \end{array}$	$\begin{array}{r} 4 \\ +9 \\ \hline \end{array}$	$\begin{array}{r} 4 \\ +7 \\ \hline \end{array}$	$\begin{array}{r} 9 \\ +3 \\ \hline \end{array}$	$\begin{array}{r} 5 \\ +6 \\ \hline \end{array}$	$\begin{array}{r} 8 \\ +2 \\ \hline \end{array}$

4

$\begin{array}{r} 6 \\ +5 \\ \hline \end{array}$	$\begin{array}{r} 7 \\ +9 \\ \hline \end{array}$	$\begin{array}{r} 9 \\ +4 \\ \hline \end{array}$	$\begin{array}{r} 8 \\ +8 \\ \hline \end{array}$	$\begin{array}{r} 9 \\ +5 \\ \hline \end{array}$	$\begin{array}{r} 4 \\ +6 \\ \hline \end{array}$

Problem Solving ■ Visual Thinking

Draw a picture of how you would use a ten frame to solve this problem.

5 Megan has 10 shells. 7 shells are pink and the rest are orange. How many orange shells does Megan have?

_______ orange shells

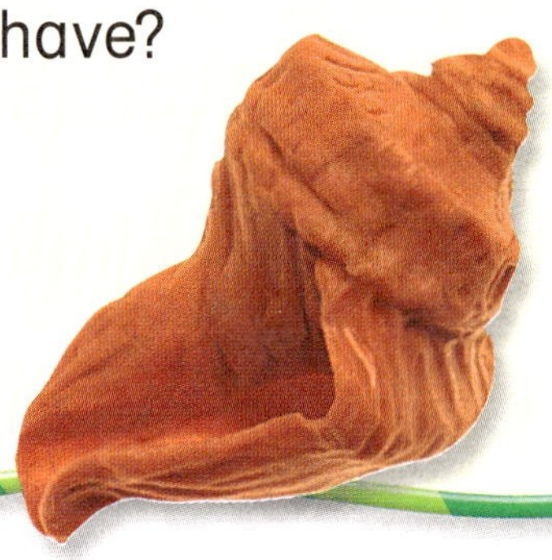

HOME ACTIVITY • Ask your child how he or she used a ten frame to find the sums on this page.

Name ______________________

Add 3 Numbers Algebra

You can add three numbers in different ways.

Choose two numbers to add first.
Look for facts you know.

$7 + 2 + 3 = \underline{12}$ → $9 + 3 = 12$

$7 + 2 + 3 = \underline{12}$ → $7 + 5 = 12$

$7 + 2 + 3 = \underline{12}$ → $10 + 2 = 12$

Circle the addends you add first. Write the sum.

	8 + 1	6 + 3
1	6 + 2 + 1 = 9	6 + 2 + 1 = 9
2	5 + 3 + 4 = ____	5 + 3 + 4 = ____
3	4 + 2 + 7 = ____	4 + 2 + 7 = ____
4	4 + 5 + 4 = ____	4 + 5 + 4 = ____
5	6 + 6 + 2 = ____	6 + 6 + 2 = ____
6	6 + 7 + 3 = ____	6 + 7 + 3 = ____

Talk About It ■ Reasoning

How do you decide which two addends to add first?

Write the sum.

1

3 →		3		3 →	
8 →	11	8 →	15	8	10
+ 7	+ 7	+ 7 →	+ 3	+ 7 →	+ 8
	18		18		18

2

5	9	1	1	6	3
4	8	7	8	1	7
+ 5	+ 1	+ 7	+ 1	+ 7	+ 2

3

2	4	2	5	5	9
7	5	8	2	3	1
+ 2	+ 4	+ 5	+ 5	+ 3	+ 7

Problem Solving ▪ Reasoning

4 Draw grapes on the 3 plates.

Ari eats the grapes on the first two plates and Jane eats the grapes on the third plate. How many grapes do they eat altogether?

_____ grapes

If Ari eats the grapes on the first plate and Jane eats the grapes on the other two plates, how many grapes do they eat altogether?

_____ grapes

Are your answers the same? Why or why not?

8 grapes

5 grapes

6 grapes

HOME ACTIVITY • Ask your child how he or she decided which two addends to add first.

CHAPTER 2

Subtraction Strategies

SCHOOL HOME CONNECTION

Dear Family,

Today we started Chapter 2. We will subtract from numbers up to 20. Here is the math vocabulary and an activity for us to do together at home

Love,

____

My Math Words

fact family

difference

Vocabulary

A **fact family** is a group of addition and subtraction facts that use the same numbers.

Here is the fact family for 7, 8, and 15:

$7 + 8 = 15$ $8 + 7 = 15$

$15 - 7 = 8$ $15 - 8 = 7$

Ask your child to write fact families.

difference The answer to a subtraction problem is the difference.

Visit *The Learning Site* for additional ideas and activities. www.harcourtschool.com

ACTIVITY

Place 20 small objects in a paper bag. Have your child remove some of the objects and say how many are left in the bag. Have your child look in the bag to count, and then have him or her say and write the subtraction sentence. Repeat with fewer than 20 objects.

Books to Share

To read about addition and subtraction with your child, look for these books in your local library.

Sea Sums,
by Joy Hulme,
Hyperion Books,
1996.

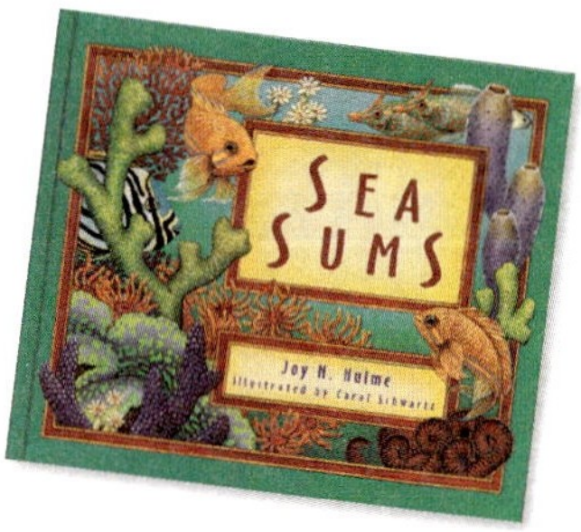

Window,
by Jeannie Baker,
HarperCollins, 1991.

Name ____________________

Subtract All or Zero

Algebra

How many boots are left?

$7 - 7 = 0$ boots

The answer when you **subtract** is called the **difference**.

How many boots are left?

$7 - 0 = 7$ boots

Subtract.

1 $3 - 3 =$ 0	2 $9 - 0 =$ 9	3 $8 - 8 =$ ____
4 $18 - 0 =$ ____	5 $14 - 0 =$ ____	6 $6 - 6 =$ ____
7 $15 - 0 =$ ____	8 $5 - 5 =$ ____	9 $1 - 1 =$ ____
10 $2 - 0 =$ ____	11 $4 - 4 =$ ____	12 $9 - 9 =$ ____

Talk About It ■ Reasoning

When you subtract 0 from a number, what will the answer always be? Why?

Subtract.

1

18	7	8	19	12	4
− 0	− 7	− 8	− 0	− 12	− 4
18	0				

2

19	10	6	3	14	5
− 19	− 0	− 0	− 3	− 0	− 5

3

2	17	3	6	10	5
− 0	− 0	− 0	− 6	− 10	− 0

4

9	11	7	12	18	8
− 9	− 0	− 0	− 0	− 0	− 0

Mixed Review

Find the sums.

5

6 + 4 = ____	3 + 9 = ____	0 + 11 = ____
4 + 6 = ____	9 + 3 = ____	11 + 0 = ____

6

0 + 8 = ____	4 + 7 = ____	6 + 0 = ____
8 + 0 = ____	7 + 4 = ____	0 + 6 = ____

HOME ACTIVITY • Show your child a group of up to 10 objects. Remove all of them or none of them. Have your child write the subtraction sentence.

Name ______________________

Count Back

What is 9 − 1?

Say 9. **Count back** 1.

8

The difference is 8.

$9 - 1 = 8$

What is 6 − 2?

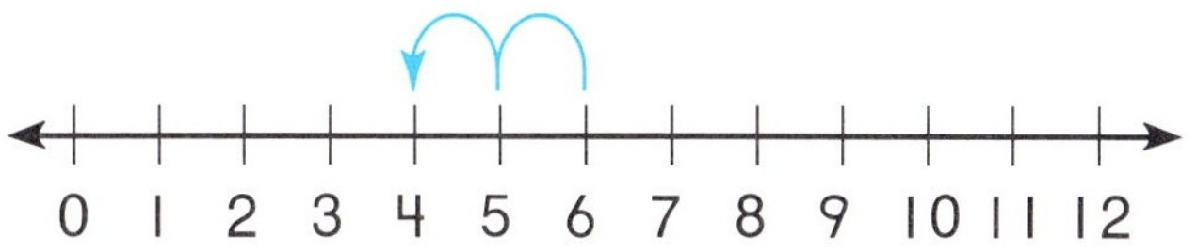

Say 6. Count back 2.

5, 4

The difference is 4.

$6 - 2 = 4$

Count back to find the difference.

1 $5 - 2 =$ 3	2 $6 - 1 =$ ____	3 $10 - 1 =$ ____
4 $11 - 2 =$ ____	5 $7 - 1 =$ ____	6 $8 - 1 =$ ____
7 $9 - 2 =$ ____	8 $11 - 1 =$ ____	9 $8 - 2 =$ ____
10 $6 - 2 =$ ____	11 $10 - 2 =$ ____	12 $5 - 1 =$ ____
13 $12 - 2 =$ ____	14 $4 - 2 =$ ____	15 $12 - 1 =$ ____

Talk About It ▪ Reasoning

Can you count back by other numbers? Give an example.

Count back to find the difference.

$\begin{array}{r} 7 \\ -3 \\ \hline ? \end{array}$

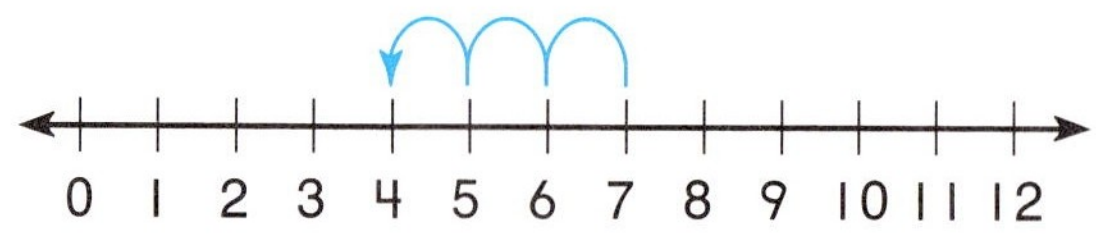

$\begin{array}{r} 7 \\ -3 \\ \hline 4 \end{array}$

1 $\begin{array}{r} 9 \\ -1 \\ \hline 8 \end{array}$ $\quad \begin{array}{r} 5 \\ -2 \\ \hline \end{array}$ $\quad \begin{array}{r} 6 \\ -2 \\ \hline \end{array}$ $\quad \begin{array}{r} 5 \\ -1 \\ \hline \end{array}$ $\quad \begin{array}{r} 7 \\ -2 \\ \hline \end{array}$

2 $\begin{array}{r} 10 \\ -2 \\ \hline \end{array}$ $\quad \begin{array}{r} 3 \\ -2 \\ \hline \end{array}$ $\quad \begin{array}{r} 6 \\ -3 \\ \hline \end{array}$ $\quad \begin{array}{r} 7 \\ -1 \\ \hline \end{array}$ $\quad \begin{array}{r} 8 \\ -1 \\ \hline \end{array}$

3 $\begin{array}{r} 8 \\ -2 \\ \hline \end{array}$ $\quad \begin{array}{r} 9 \\ -3 \\ \hline \end{array}$ $\quad \begin{array}{r} 11 \\ -3 \\ \hline \end{array}$ $\quad \begin{array}{r} 4 \\ -3 \\ \hline \end{array}$ $\quad \begin{array}{r} 10 \\ -1 \\ \hline \end{array}$

4 $\begin{array}{r} 11 \\ -2 \\ \hline \end{array}$ $\quad \begin{array}{r} 7 \\ -3 \\ \hline \end{array}$ $\quad \begin{array}{r} 12 \\ -3 \\ \hline \end{array}$ $\quad \begin{array}{r} 8 \\ -3 \\ \hline \end{array}$ $\quad \begin{array}{r} 4 \\ -1 \\ \hline \end{array}$

Algebra

5 Write the missing numbers.

9 − 1 = 8	10 − 1 = 9	11 − 1 = 10
9 − 2 = ___	10 − 2 = ___	11 − 2 = ___
9 − ___ = ___	10 − ___ = ___	11 − ___ = ___
9 − ___ = ___	10 − ___ = ___	11 − ___ = ___

HOME ACTIVITY • Have your child tell you how to count back to solve 10 − 3.

Name ____________________

Think Addition to Subtract

Hands On

Use cubes.
Add or subtract.

1 $6 + 5 =$ ___ $11 - 5 =$ ___	**2** $4 + 3 =$ ___ $7 - 3 =$ ___	**3** $3 + 7 =$ ___ $10 - 7 =$ ___
4 $9 + 7 =$ ___ $16 - 7 =$ ___	**5** $8 + 3 =$ ___ $11 - 3 =$ ___	**6** $5 + 8 =$ ___ $13 - 8 =$ ___
7 $9 + 8 =$ ___ $17 - 8 =$ ___	**8** $6 + 8 =$ ___ $14 - 8 =$ ___	**9** $8 + 7 =$ ___ $15 - 7 =$ ___

Talk About It ■ **Reasoning**

How does knowing $7 + 5 = 12$ help you solve $12 - 5$?

Add or subtract.

1 $4 + 7 =$ 11　　　　$11 - 7 =$ 4

2 $7 + 5 =$ ____　　　　$12 - 5 =$ ____

3 $9 + 6 =$ ____　　　　$15 - 6 =$ ____

4 $6 + 4 =$ ____　　　　$10 - 4 =$ ____

5 $9 + 5 =$ ____　　　　$14 - 5 =$ ____

6 $8 + 7 =$ ____　　　　$15 - 7 =$ ____

Problem Solving • Application

Solve.

7 Mary got a toy turtle for 9¢ and a toy fish for 8¢. How much money did she spend? ____¢

8 Nathan had 17¢. He spent 8¢. How much money did he have left? ____¢

HOME ACTIVITY • Have your child explain how knowing $5 + 6 = 11$ helps him or her to solve $11 - 5 = 6$.

Name ______________________________

Fact Families

6 blue 7 red

13 in all

6, 7, and 13 are the numbers in this **fact family**.

6 + 7 = 13	7 + 6 = 13
13 − 6 = 7	13 − 7 = 6

Write the fact family for the set of numbers.

1 8 9

17

_____ + _____ = _____ _____ + _____ = _____

_____ − _____ = _____ _____ _____ = _____

2 6 8

14

_____ + _____ = _____ _____ + _____ = _____

_____ − _____ = _____ _____ − _____ = _____

Talk About It ■ **Reasoning**

How many different number sentences can you write for the set of numbers 6, 6, and 12? Why?

Write the fact family for the set of numbers.

1 Numbers: 12, 8, 4

$4 + 8 = 12$ $8 + 4 = 12$

$12 - 8 = 4$ $12 - 4 = 8$

2 Numbers: 16, 9, 7

$\square + \square = \square$ $\square + \square = \square$

$\square - \square = \square$ $\square - \square = \square$

3 Numbers: 15, 7, 8

$\square + \square = \square$ $\square + \square = \square$

$\square - \square = \square$ $\square - \square = \square$

4 Numbers: 11, 4, 7

$\square + \square = \square$ $\square + \square = \square$

$\square - \square = \square$ $\square - \square = \square$

HOME ACTIVITY • Give your child the numbers 5, 7, and 12, and have him or her write the fact family.

Name ______________________________

UNDERSTAND › PLAN › SOLVE › CHECK

Which statements equal 9?
Which statements do not?

9	
(18 − 9)	
(14 − 5)	
~~13 − 5~~	13 − 4
~~2 + 2 + 4~~	2 + 2 + 5
(3 + 2 + 4)	
(16 − 7)	
(3 + 3 + 3)	

Circle the statements that equal the number at the top. Cross out others. Correct those statements.

1

12
~~6 + 5~~
(5 + 5 + 2)
3 + 9
8 + 4
3 + 7
6 + 6

2

7
0 + 10
2 + 5
3 + 0 + 5
16 − 9
15 − 8
4 + 3

Circle the statements that equal the number at the top.
Cross out the others. Correct those statements.

1

14
14 + 0
7 + 9
17 − 3
7 + 4 + 2
14 − 0
7 + 7

2

11
1 + 5 + 5
5 + 6
12 − 1
6 + 2 + 2
6 + 6
14 − 3

3

10
13 − 3
10 + 1
5 + 5
7 + 4
15 − 5
11 − 1

4

6
4 + 2 + 2
6 − 0
10 − 3
12 − 7
3 + 3
5 + 1

Algebra

Write + or −. Make each equal 6.

5 13 ◯ 7 4 ◯ 2 14 ◯ 8 2 ◯ 2 ◯ 2

HOME ACTIVITY • Ask your child to show three ways to get a sum of 10 and three ways to get a difference of 10.

Name ______________________

CHECK ■ Concepts and Skills

Subtract.

1 3 − 3 = ____ 7 − 0 = ____ 8 − 0 = ____

2 9 − 9 = ____ 11 − 0 = ____ 12 − 12 = ____

Count back to find the difference.

3 7 − 2 = ____ 8 − 1 = ____ 5 − 3 = ____

Use [cube]. Add or subtract.

4

$$\begin{array}{r} 7 \\ +2 \\ \hline \end{array} \quad \begin{array}{r} 9 \\ -2 \\ \hline \end{array} \quad \begin{array}{r} 6 \\ +3 \\ \hline \end{array} \quad \begin{array}{r} 9 \\ -6 \\ \hline \end{array}$$

5 Write the fact family for the set of numbers.

6 5

11

____ + ____ = ____

____ − ____ = ____

____ + ____ = ____

____ − ____ = ____

CHECK ■ Problem Solving

6 Circle the statements that equal the number at the top. Cross out the others. Correct those statements.

8
4 + 5
10 − 2
6 + 2 + 2
8 + 0
9 − 1
16 − 8

Name ______________________

Choose the best answer for questions 1–5.

1 $9 - 9 =$ ____

○ 0 ○ 9 ○ 18 ○ 19

2 $5 - 0 =$ ____

○ 0 ○ 5 ○ 10 ○ 11

3 Which addition fact can help you solve this subtraction fact?

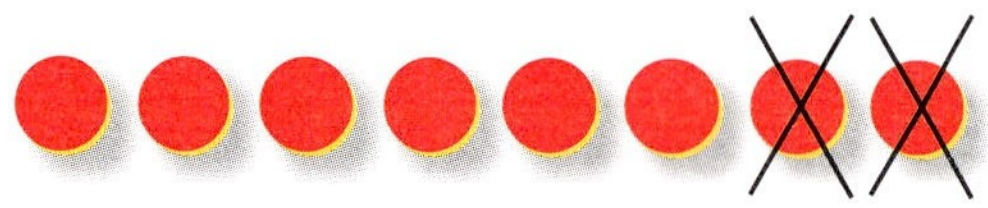

$8 - 2 = 6$

○ $3 + 5 = 8$ ○ $7 + 1 = 8$ ○ $6 + 2 = 8$ ○ $6 - 2 = 4$

4 Which is **not** a way to make 13?

○ $14 - 1$ ○ $6 + 7$ ○ $10 + 3$ ○ $12 - 1$

5 Ricco sees 14 cows in a field. Five of the cows are brown. The rest are white. How many cows are white?

○ 8 ○ 9 ○ 10 ○ 19

Show What You Know

6 Color some of the cubes blue and some red.
Write the number sentences that are in the fact family.

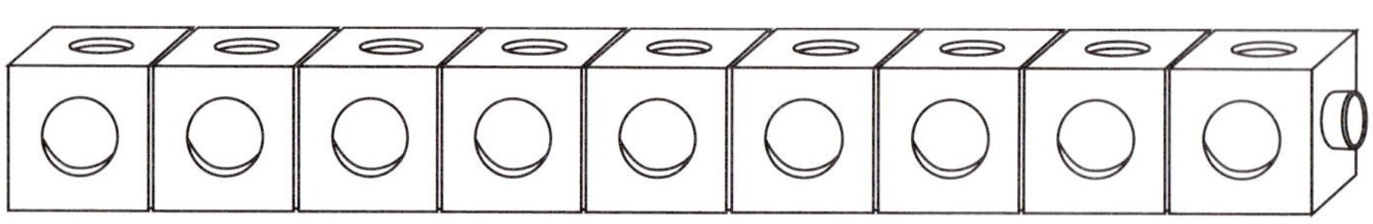

____ ○ ____ ○ ____   ____ ○ ____ ○ ____

____ ○ ____ ○ ____   ____ ○ ____ ○ ____

CHAPTER 3

Addition and Subtraction Practice

Each team has 10 runners. How many from each team have not crossed the finish line?

SCHOOL HOME CONNECTION

Dear Family,

Today we started Chapter 3. We will practice addition and subtraction strategies. Here is the math vocabulary and an activity for us to do together at home.

Love,

____

My Math Words

missing number

Vocabulary

A **missing number** is a number missing from the first part of an addition or subtraction sentence.

For example, in 7 + ____ = 15, the missing number is 8.

Give your child some problems like this to solve.

Visit *The Learning Site* for additional ideas and activities. www.harcourtschool.com

ACTIVITY

Read a book to your child, and ask him or her to make up a number problem about the characters in the story. Your child should draw a picture of the problem and then write a number sentence to solve.

Books to Share

To read about addition and subtraction with your child, look for these books in your local library.

Ready, Set, Hop!,
by Stuart J. Murphy,
HarperCollins, 1996.

Animals on Board,
by Stuart J. Murphy,
HarperCollins, 1998.

Each Orange Had 8 Slices,
by Paul Giganti Jr.,
William Morrow & Company, 1999.

Name ______________________

Addition Facts

Add in any order.

$4 + 6 = 10$
and
$6 + 4 = 10$

Use doubles.

$9 + 9 = 18$
1 more
$9 + 10 = 19$

Make a ten.

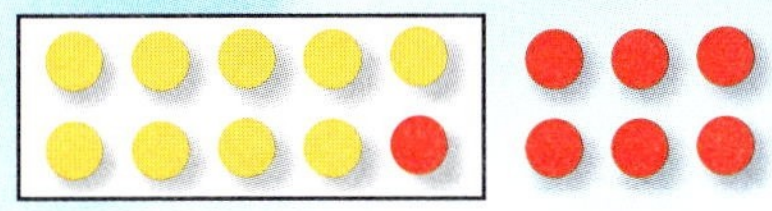

$10 + 6 = 16$
so
$9 + 7 = 16$

Count on.

$8 + 3 = 11$

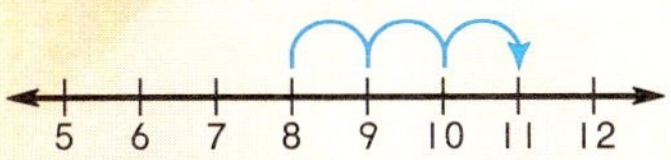

Say 8. Count on 3.
9, 10, 11

Add zero.

$10 + 0 = 10$

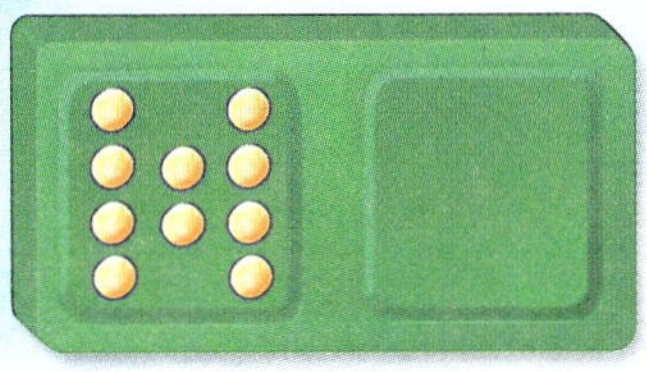

Add three numbers.

$6 + 4 + 3 = 13$

$10 + 3 = 13$

Write the sum.

1 $10 + 1 = $ 11 $\quad 1 + 10 = $ ___ $\quad 7 + 5 = $ ___ $\quad 5 + 7 = $ ___ $\quad 8 + 2 = $ ___ $\quad 2 + 8 = $ ___

2 $7 + 7 = $ ___ $\quad 7 + 8 = $ ___ $\quad 8 + 8 = $ ___ $\quad 9 + 8 = $ ___ $\quad 9 + 9 = $ ___ $\quad 9 + 10 = $ ___

3 $10 + 3 = $ ___ $\quad 8 + 2 = $ ___ $\quad 9 + 1 = $ ___ $\quad 9 + 3 = $ ___ $\quad 7 + 1 = $ ___ $\quad 6 + 0 = $ ___

4 $7 + 2 + 5 = $ ______

5 $4 + 6 + 6 = $ ______

Talk About It ■ Reasoning

Choose one of the rows. What strategy did you use to solve each problem? Explain your thinking.

Write the sum.

1

Use doubles.	
8	16
5	
10	
9	

2

Use doubles plus one.	
6	
8	
4	

3

Add 0.	
12	
5	
10	
7	

4

Count on 1.	
7	
4	
11	
9	

5

Count on 2.	
8	
10	
7	
5	

6

Count on 3.	
7	
8	
9	
10	

Problem Solving ▪ Reasoning

7 Sharon made a ten to find the sums. What mistake did she make each time? Correct her mistakes.

$$\begin{array}{r} 9 \\ +8 \\ \hline 16 \end{array} \qquad \begin{array}{r} 9 \\ +5 \\ \hline 13 \end{array} \qquad \begin{array}{r} 9 \\ +6 \\ \hline 14 \end{array}$$

HOME ACTIVITY • Each day, work with your child to practice facts with a given sum. For example, on Monday, practice all of the facts with a sum of 15.

Name ______________________________ **Missing Numbers** Hands On Algebra

$7 + \underline{\ ?\ } = 15$ $\qquad$ $15 - 7 = \underline{\ ?\ }$

$7 + \underline{\ 8\ } = 15$ $\qquad$ $15 - 7 = \underline{\ 8\ }$

Write the missing number. Use counters if you need to.

1. $6 + \underline{\ 4\ } = 10$ $\qquad$ $10 - 6 = \underline{\qquad}$

2. $\underline{\qquad} + 9 = 12$ $\qquad$ $12 - 9 = \underline{\qquad}$

3. $7 + \underline{\qquad} = 14$ $\qquad$ $14 - 7 = \underline{\qquad}$

4. $\underline{\qquad} + 5 = 11$ $\qquad$ $11 - 5 = \underline{\qquad}$

5. $8 + \underline{\qquad} = 16$ $\qquad$ $16 - 8 = \underline{\qquad}$

6. $\underline{\qquad} + 9 = 13$ $\qquad$ $13 - 9 = \underline{\qquad}$

7. $6 + \underline{\qquad} = 15$ $\qquad$ $15 - 6 = \underline{\qquad}$

Talk About It ■ **Reasoning**

Glen had 15 marbles. He gave some to a friend.
If he has 9 left, how many did he give to his friend? How do you know?

Write the missing number.
Use counters if you need to.

1. $4 + \underline{\ 8\ } = 12$ $\qquad$ $12 - 4 = \_\_\_\_$

2. $\_\_\_\_ + 7 = 10$ $\qquad$ $10 - 7 = \_\_\_\_$

3. $9 + \_\_\_\_ = 16$ $\qquad$ $16 - 9 = \_\_\_\_$

4. $\_\_\_\_ + 4 = 11$ $\qquad$ $11 - 4 = \_\_\_\_$

5. $6 + \_\_\_\_ = 14$ $\qquad$ $14 - 6 = \_\_\_\_$

6. $\_\_\_\_ + 9 = 18$ $\qquad$ $18 - 9 = \_\_\_\_$

7. $6 + \_\_\_\_ = 14$ $\qquad$ $14 - 6 = \_\_\_\_$

8. $4 + \_\_\_\_ = 13$ $\qquad$ $13 - 4 = \_\_\_\_$

Algebra

Solve.

9. 16 − ■ = 8

■ = ____

10. 5 + ■ = 12

■ = ____

11. 13 − ■ = 9

■ = ____

HOME ACTIVITY • Put 20 small items in a bag. Have your child remove some, count them, and tell how many are left in the bag. Repeat.

Name ______________________

Subtraction Facts

There are many ways to subtract.

Subtract zero and all.

$$\begin{array}{r} 13 \\ -\ 0 \\ \hline 13 \end{array} \qquad \begin{array}{r} 10 \\ -10 \\ \hline 0 \end{array}$$

Count back.

$$\begin{array}{r} 12 \\ -\ 3 \\ \hline 9 \end{array}$$

Say 12.
Count back 3.
11, 10, 9

Use doubles.

$$\begin{array}{r} 9 \\ +9 \\ \hline 18 \end{array} \quad \text{so} \quad \begin{array}{r} 18 \\ -\ 9 \\ \hline 9 \end{array}$$

Use addition.

$8 + 6 = \underline{14}$

$14 - 6 = \underline{8}$

Subtract.
Choose a strategy.

1

$$\begin{array}{r} 9 \\ -\ 1 \\ \hline 8 \end{array} \quad \begin{array}{r} 10 \\ -\ 5 \\ \hline \end{array} \quad \begin{array}{r} 13 \\ -\ 5 \\ \hline \end{array} \quad \begin{array}{r} 9 \\ -3 \\ \hline \end{array} \quad \begin{array}{r} 8 \\ -2 \\ \hline \end{array} \quad \begin{array}{r} 15 \\ -15 \\ \hline \end{array}$$

2

$$\begin{array}{r} 10 \\ -\ 3 \\ \hline \end{array} \quad \begin{array}{r} 15 \\ -\ 0 \\ \hline \end{array} \quad \begin{array}{r} 12 \\ -12 \\ \hline \end{array} \quad \begin{array}{r} 11 \\ -\ 1 \\ \hline \end{array} \quad \begin{array}{r} 12 \\ -\ 0 \\ \hline \end{array} \quad \begin{array}{r} 16 \\ -\ 8 \\ \hline \end{array}$$

3

$$\begin{array}{r} 11 \\ -\ 3 \\ \hline \end{array} \quad \begin{array}{r} 7 \\ -1 \\ \hline \end{array} \quad \begin{array}{r} 15 \\ -\ 8 \\ \hline \end{array} \quad \begin{array}{r} 14 \\ -\ 3 \\ \hline \end{array} \quad \begin{array}{r} 17 \\ -\ 9 \\ \hline \end{array} \quad \begin{array}{r} 18 \\ -\ 9 \\ \hline \end{array}$$

Talk About It ■ Reasoning

For which problems did you use doubles?
Explain your thinking.

Solve.
Color the doubles facts (blue crayon).
Color the count-back facts (orange crayon).
Color the all and zero facts any way you like.

$$\begin{array}{r}18\\-\ 9\\\hline\end{array}\quad\begin{array}{r}13\\-\ 0\\\hline\end{array}\quad\begin{array}{r}12\\-\ 6\\\hline\end{array}\quad\begin{array}{r}13\\-\ 3\\\hline\end{array}\quad\begin{array}{r}14\\-\ 7\\\hline\end{array}$$

$$\begin{array}{r}14\\-\ 0\\\hline\end{array}\quad\begin{array}{r}16\\-\ 8\\\hline\end{array}\quad\begin{array}{r}15\\-\ 1\\\hline\end{array}\quad\begin{array}{r}17\\-\ 2\\\hline\end{array}$$

$$\begin{array}{r}10\\-\ 5\\\hline\end{array}\quad\begin{array}{r}19\\-19\\\hline\end{array}\quad\begin{array}{r}15\\-15\\\hline\end{array}\quad\begin{array}{r}18\\-\ 3\\\hline\end{array}$$

Problem Solving ■ Visual Thinking

Use the picture to solve.

1. What if there were 8 fewer balls? How many balls would there be? _______ balls

2. What if there were 5 fewer balls? How many balls would there be? _______ balls

HOME ACTIVITY • Each day, work with your child to practice subtracting from a given number. For example, on Monday, practice subtracting from 15.

Name ______________________________

UNDERSTAND PLAN SOLVE CHECK

There were 15 girls at the game.
Then 6 girls went home.
How many girls were still at the game?

UNDERSTAND

What do you want to find out?

PLAN

You can write a number sentence to solve the problem.

SOLVE

You can draw a picture or make a model.
Then write a number sentence to solve.

15 ○ 6 = 9 girls

CHECK

Does your answer make sense? Explain.

Draw a picture or make a model.
Write a number sentence to solve.

1. After the game, 9 girls and 7 boys had a picnic. How many children were at the picnic?

_____ ○ _____ = _____ children

2. In the yard, 9 girls played catch. Then 8 more girls joined them. How many girls played catch?

_____ ○ _____ = _____ girls

Draw a picture or make a model.
Write a number sentence to solve.

1. At the game, 7 girls and 5 boys cheered. How many children cheered at the game?

   7 ⊕ 5 = 12 children

2. There were 5 wooden bats and 8 metal bats. How many bats were there in all?

   ____ ◯ ____ = ____ bats

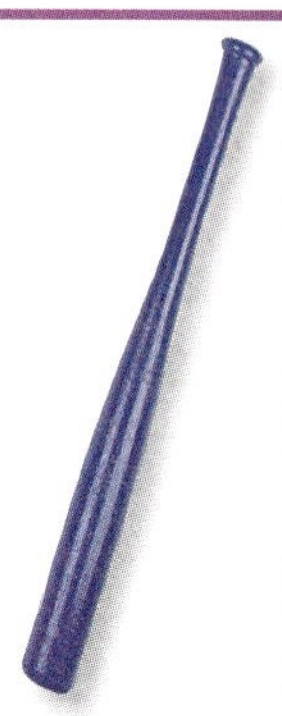

3. There were 16 girls and 8 boys playing ball. How many more girls than boys were playing ball?

   ____ ◯ ____ = ____ more girls

4. At the game, 4 girls sat together. Then 9 more girls joined them. How many girls were sitting together?

   ____ ◯ ____ = ____ girls

Math Journal

Write About It

Make up an addition story or a subtraction story.
Draw a picture to show your story.

HOME ACTIVITY • **Make up a story problem for your child to solve.**

Name ______________________

CHECK ▪ Concepts and Skills

Write the sum.

1

4	6	0	5	9	1
+ 4	+ 3	+ 2	+ 3	+ 1	+ 6

2 $4 + 7 + 4 =$ ______ $1 + 9 + 3 =$ ______

Write the missing number. Use counters if you need to.

3

$7 +$ ______ $= 13$

$13 - 7 =$ ______

4

$8 +$ ______ $= 11$

$11 - 8 =$ ______

5

______ $+ 9 = 12$

$12 - 9 =$ ______

Subtract. Choose a strategy.

6

5	10	7	14	7	9
− 0	− 5	− 7	− 7	− 2	− 2

CHECK ▪ Problem Solving

Draw a picture or make a model.
Write a number sentence to solve.

7 There are 9 apples and 4 oranges in the bowl. How many apples and oranges are in the bowl?

______ ◯ ______ = ______

Name ______________________________

Choose the best answer for questions 1–7.

1 $5 + 3 = \_\_\_\_$

1 ○ 8 ○ 9 ○ 10 ○

2 $9 - 3 = \_\_\_\_$

6 ○ 7 ○ 8 ○ 9 ○

3 $3 + 7 + 6 = \_\_\_\_$

9 ○ 10 ○ 15 ○ 16 ○

4 $11 - \_\_\_\_ = 11$

0 ○ 10 ○ 11 ○ 19 ○

5 $8 + \_\_\_\_ = 11$

1 ○ 2 ○ 3 ○ 4 ○

6 $17 + 0 = \_\_\_\_$

0 ○ 7 ○ 17 ○ 19 ○

7 There are 9 kick balls and 5 soccer balls in a bag.
How many kick balls and soccer balls are there in the bag?

4 ○ 6 ○ 13 ○ 14 ○

Show What You Know

8 Write a number less than 9 in the blank.
Color the marbles to match the problem.
Write a number sentence.

Joe had ______ marbles.
He found some more marbles.
Then he had 12 marbles.
How many marbles did he find?

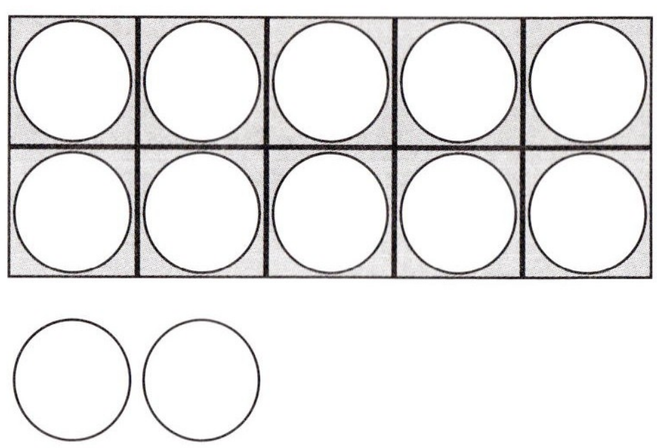

______ ◯ ______ ◯ ______ marbles

Winter Is Near!

written by Maria Kathe
illustrated by David Slonim

This book will help me review addition and subtraction facts.

This book belongs to ____________________.

A

Winter is near. A few chipmunks and a squirrel have been gathering food in the forest.

“Look! We found 8 big seeds,” said a chipmunk.

“I found 6,” added the squirrel. “We can put them away to eat this winter.”

How many seeds did the animals find?

$8 + 6 = \_\_\_\_\_$

“We have so many seeds,” said one chipmunk. “Maybe we should share with the mice in the field. They might need some food this winter.”

"Good idea!" said the squirrel. "I can give the 6 seeds I found to the mice. We can keep the ones you found for ourselves."

How many seeds did the animals keep?

14 – 6 = _____

"How about some walnuts?
We love to eat nuts in the winter,"
said a chipmunk.

"I saw 8 on one side of the fence and
8 on the other side," said the squirrel.
"We'll keep 8 and give the rest to
the mice."

How many walnuts did they find?

$8 + 8 =$ _____

How many did they keep?

$16 - 8 =$ _____

"Surprise!" said the chipmunks.
The squirrel said, "Winter is near!
We brought you some food to help
make your winter nice."

"Thank you!" said the mother field mouse.
"The nicest part of winter is friends like you.
Come in and get warm. Winter is here!"

CHAPTER 4 Numbers to 100

SCHOOL HOME CONNECTION

Dear Family,

Today we started Chapter 4. We will read, write, and use numbers to 100. We will begin to learn about place value. Here is the math vocabulary and an activity for us to do together at home.

Love,

____

My Math Words

tens and ones
digits

Vocabulary

tens and ones The value of the digits in two-digit numbers.

3 tens 4 ones = 34

digits 0, 1, 2, 3, 4, 5, 6, 7, 8, and 9 are digits.

ACTIVITY

Give your child between 11 and 99 small objects. Have him or her group the objects into tens and say and write how many groups of ten there are, how many ones are left over, and the total number of objects. Repeat.

Books to Share

To read about numbers to 100 with your child, look for these books in your local library.

One Hundred Hungry Ants,
by Elinor J. Pinczes,
Houghton Mifflin, 1993.

Betcha!,
by Stuart J. Murphy,
HarperCollins, 1997.

Emily's First 100 Days of School,
by Rosemary Wells,
Hyperion, 2000.

Visit *The Learning Site* for additional ideas and activities. www.harcourtschool.com

Name ______________________________

Tens

1 ten = 10 ones

Circle groups of ten. Write how many tens. Then write how many ones.

1

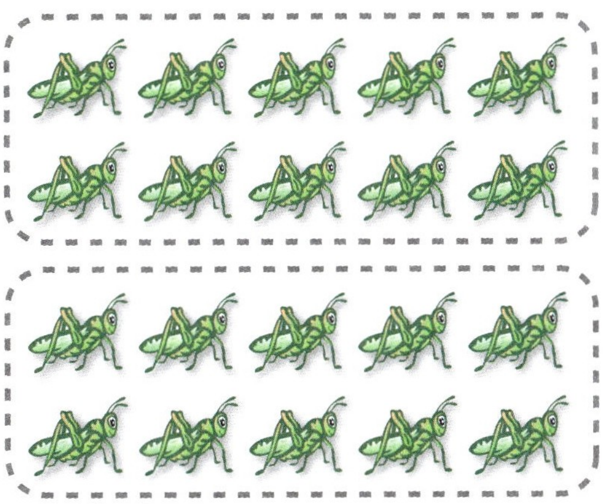

2 tens = 20 ones

2

______ tens = ______ ones

3

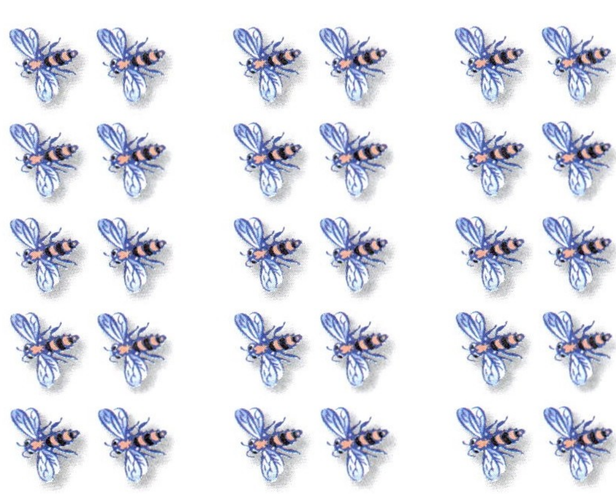

______ tens = ______ ones

4

______ tens = ______ ones

Talk About It ▪ Reasoning

What patterns do you see in the numbers that name the tens and the ones?

Count the spots. Write how many tens.
Then write how many ones.

1 

5 tens = 50 ones

2 

______ tens = ______ ones

3 

______ tens = ______ ones

4 

______ tens = ______ ones

5 

______ tens = ______ ones

Problem Solving ▪ Visual Thinking

6 Which is easier to count? Circle it. Tell why.

HOME ACTIVITY • Ask your child to set out small objects in groups of ten and tell you first how many tens and then how many ones there are.

Name ______________________________

Tens and Ones

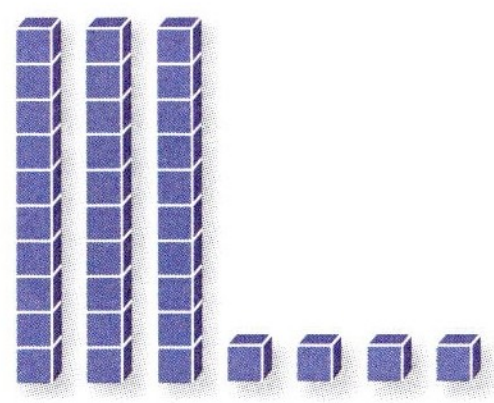

3 tens 4 ones = 34

30 + 4 = 34

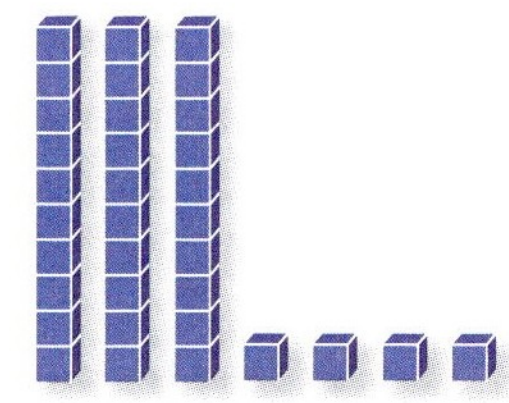

34

Write how many tens and ones in three different ways.

1 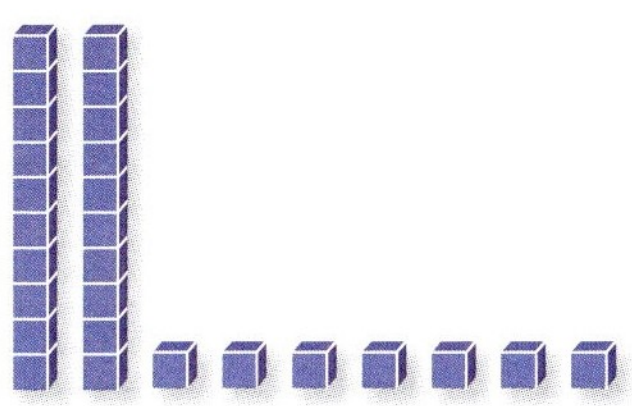

2 tens 7 ones = 27

20 + 7 = 27

27

2 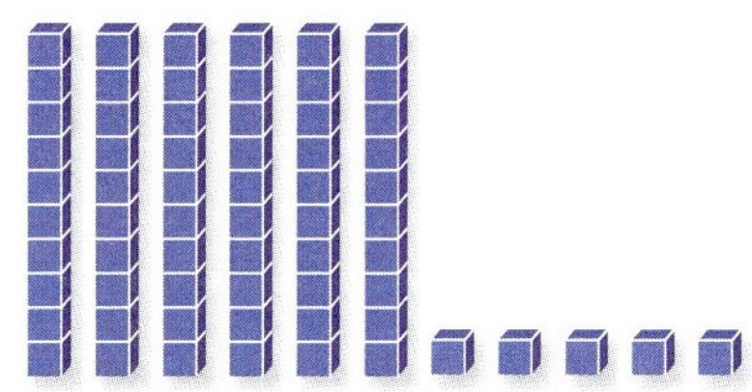

____ tens ____ ones = ____

____ + ____ = ____

____

3 

____ tens ____ ones = ____

____ + ____ = ____

____

4 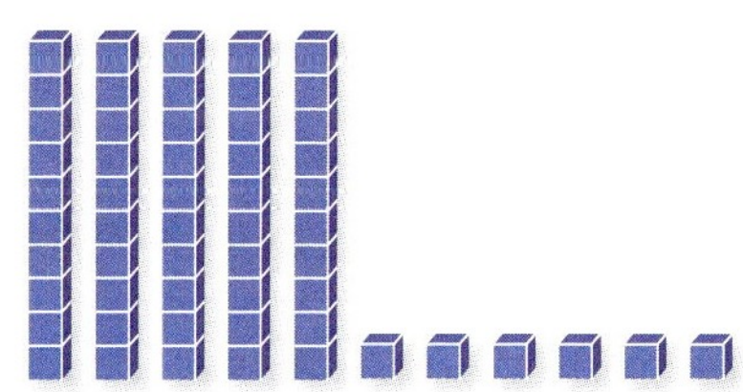

____ tens ____ ones = ____

____ + ____ = ____

____

Talk About It ■ Reasoning

What does the 6 stand for in 16 and in 61?

Write how many tens and ones in three different ways.

1 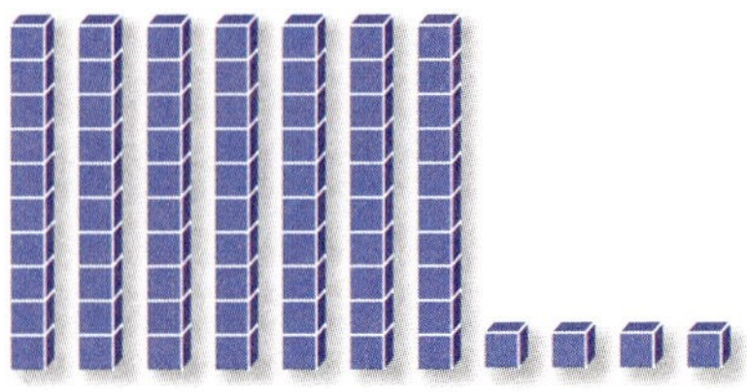

7 tens 4 ones = 74

70 + 4 = 74

74

2 

____ tens ____ ones = ____

____ + ____ = ____

____

3 

____ tens ____ ones = ____

____ + ____ = ____

____

4 

____ tens ____ ones = ____

____ + ____ = ____

____

Problem Solving ▪ Application

Draw a model to solve.

5 Joe counts his marbles. He puts them in 4 groups of ten and has 6 marbles left over. How many marbles does he have?

______ marbles

HOME ACTIVITY • **Ask your child to set out 99 or fewer small objects in groups of tens and ones and tell you the number.**

Name ______________________________

Understand Place Value

0, 1, 2, 3, 4, 5, 6, 7, 8, and 9 are **digits**.
Digits are used to write numbers.

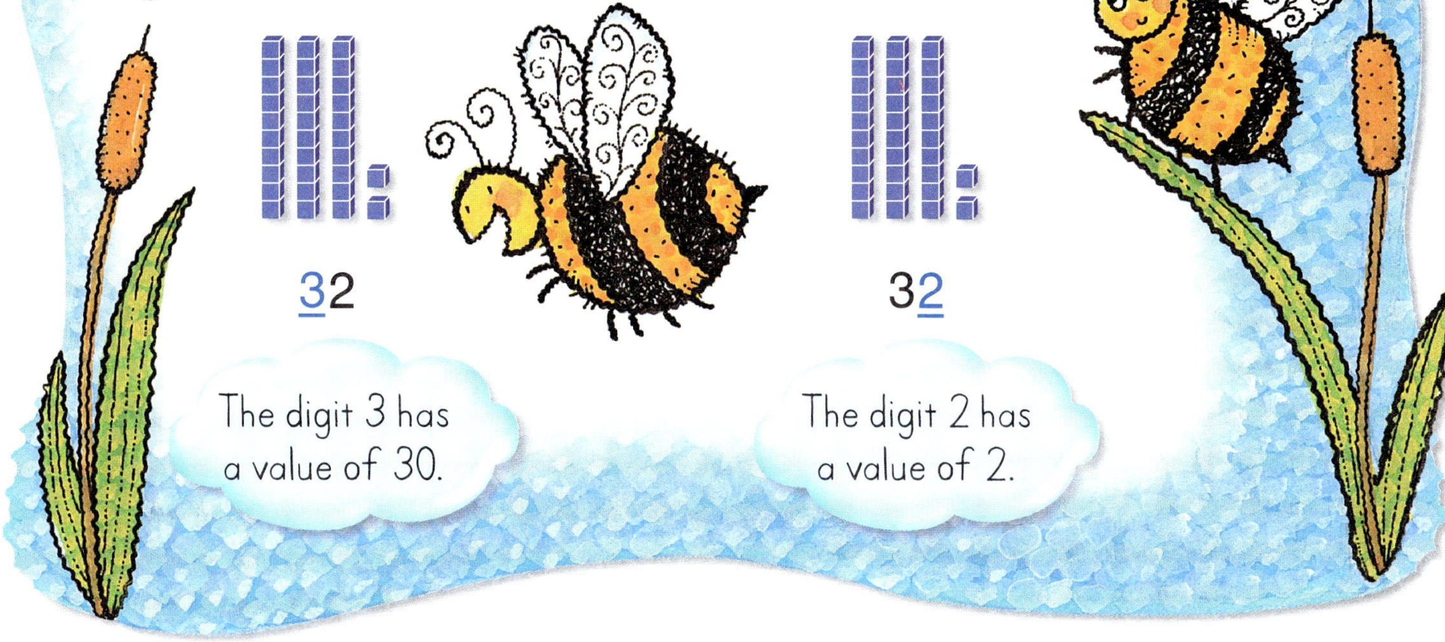

Circle the value of the blue digit.

1 64

6 or 60

2 53

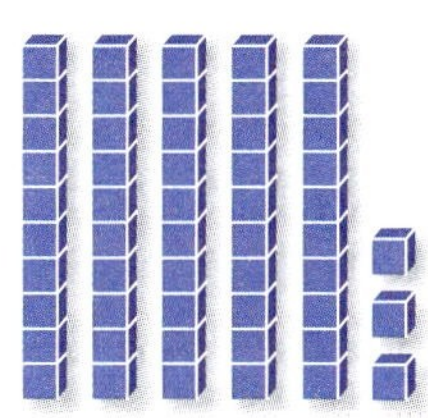

3 or 30

3 46

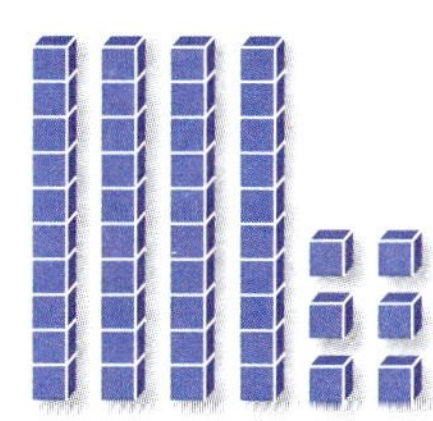

6 or 60

4 23

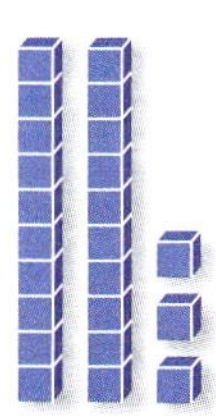

2 or 20

5 75

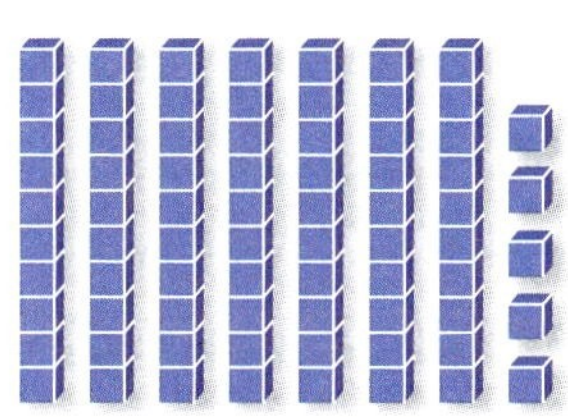

5 or 50

6 17

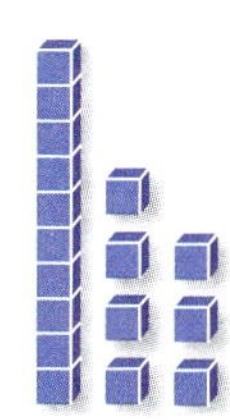

1 or 10

Talk About It ▪ Reasoning

How would you put these numbers in order from least to greatest? 5 51 15 Explain.

Circle the value of the blue digit.

1. 73 3 or 30	2. 57 5 or 50	3. 38 8 or 80
4. 78 7 or 70	5. 19 9 or 90	6. 83 8 or 80
7. 62 6 or 60	8. 98 9 or 90	9. 45 5 or 50
10. 12 1 or 10	11. 36 6 or 60	12. 23 2 or 20
13. 41 1 or 10	14. 27 2 or 20	15. 16 1 or 10
16. 93 9 or 90	17. 75 5 or 50	18. 86 6 or 60

Problem Solving ■ Number Sense

Circle the number that has the same value.

19. 6 ones 7 tens 76 or 67	20. 4 tens 3 ones 34 or 43	21. 2 ones 8 tens 82 or 28
22. 3 tens 5 ones 35 or 53	23. 9 ones 5 tens 95 or 59	24. 4 ones 1 ten 14 or 41

HOME ACTIVITY • On a calendar, point to number 23. Ask your child to tell the value of the 2 in it. (20) Then point to number 2 on the calendar and ask its value. (2) Repeat with 30 and 3.

Name ______________________________

Read and Write Numbers

tens		ones		teen words	
10 ten	20 twenty	1 one	2 two	11 eleven	12 twelve
30 thirty	40 forty	3 three	4 four	13 thirteen	14 fourteen
50 fifty	60 sixty	5 five	6 six	15 fifteen	16 sixteen
70 seventy	80 eighty	7 seven	8 eight	17 seventeen	18 eighteen
90 ninety		9 nine		19 nineteen	

Read the number.
Write the number in different ways.

1. ninety-six

9 tens 6 ones

90 + 6

96

2. eighteen

_____ ten _____ ones

_____ + _____

_____

3. sixty-two

_____ tens _____ ones

_____ + _____

_____

4. fourteen

_____ tens _____ ones

_____ + _____

_____

5. seventy

_____ tens _____ ones

_____ + _____

_____

6. eighty-one

_____ tens _____ one

_____ + _____

_____

7. twenty-three

_____ tens _____ ones

_____ + _____

_____

8. fifty-seven

_____ tens _____ ones

_____ + _____

_____

9. thirteen

_____ ten _____ ones

_____ + _____

_____

Talk About It ■ **Reasoning**

In what three ways can you show the number 85?

Read the number.
Write the number in different ways.

1 twenty-five

2 tens 5 ones

20 + 5

25

2 thirty-three

____ tens ____ ones

____ + ____

____

3 ninety-one

____ tens ____ one

____ + ____

____

4 fifty-eight

____ tens ____ ones

____ + ____

____

5 forty-seven

____ tens ____ ones

____ + ____

____

6 seventy-four

____ tens ____ ones

____ + ____

____

Mixed Review

About how many are in the first jar?
Circle the best estimate.

7

more than 50

about 50

HOME ACTIVITY • Name any number from 1 to 99, for example, 76. Have your child write that number as tens and ones (7 tens 6 ones), in expanded notation (70 + 6), and as a number in standard form (76).

Name ____________________

UNDERSTAND › PLAN › SOLVE › CHECK

Carol carries her books to school. About how many books could Carol carry?

(5) 50 100

Carol could carry about <u>5</u> books.

Circle the most reasonable estimate.

1. The Smiths went away on a short vacation. About how many days might they be away?

5 50 100

2. Carmen put pennies in this jar. About how many pennies might she have?

3 30 100

3. Larry has a handful of marbles. About how many marbles might he have?

10 40 100

4. Hojin has a small fishbowl. About how many fish might he have?

5 20 100

Circle the most reasonable estimate.

1. Luis builds a tower with blocks. About how many blocks might he use?

10 60 100

2. Emma invited the entire class to her party. About how many children might that be?

5 20 100

3. Greg carried a bag of apples. About how many apples might be in the bag?

10 50 100

4. Jenny buys a bunch of grapes. About how many grapes might be in a bunch?

5 30 100

5. Kim's stamp book is full. About how many stamps might she have?

10 20 100

6. All the second-grade classes will go on a trip. About how many buses might they use?

5 50 100

Write About It

Write a story problem like the ones on this page. Ask a classmate to solve your problem.

HOME ACTIVITY • Ask your child how many apples you should buy at the store— 10, 40, or 100. Talk about which answer makes the most sense.

Name ______________________________

CHECK ■ Concepts and Skills

Count the spots.
Write how many tens.
Then write how many ones.

1 ______ tens = ______ ones

Circle the value of the blue digit.

2 24

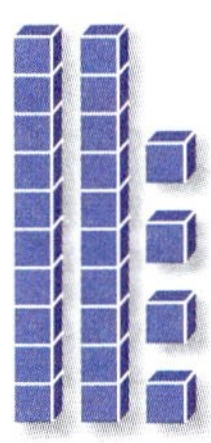

4 or 40

Circle the value of the blue digit.

3 37

7 or 70

12

1 or 10

Read the number. Write the number in different ways.

4 twenty-four

______ tens ______ ones

______ + ______

______

5 thirty-seven

______ tens ______ ones

______ + ______

______

CHECK ■ Problem Solving

Circle the most reasonable estimate.

6 Akio packs apples in his family's lunches.
About how many apples might he pack?

5 30 100

Name ______________________________

Choose the best answer for questions 1–4.

1 There are 10 spots on each ladybug.
How many spots are there in all?

60	70	80	90
○	○	○	○

2 What is the value of the underlined digit?

$\underline{7}3$

3	7	30	70
○	○	○	○

3 Which number matches the words?

thirty-one

31	13	3	30
○	○	○	○

4 Which addition fact can help you solve this subtraction fact?

$12 - 3 = 9$

$9 - 3 = 6$	$4 + 8 = 12$	$9 + 3 = 12$	$7 + 5 = 12$
○	○	○	○

Show What You Know

5 Draw blocks. Show tens and ones.
Write the number in three different ways.

____ tens ____ ones

____ + ____

____

CHAPTER 5

Number Patterns, Compare and Order

SCHOOL HOME CONNECTION

Dear Family,
Today we started Chapter 5. We will compare numbers and put them in order. We will also learn about number patterns. Here is the math vocabulary and an activity for us to do together at home.

Love,

____

My Math Words
greater than >
less than <

Vocabulary

greater than (>) and **less than** (<)
Symbols used to compare two numbers.

$49 > 34 \qquad 34 < 49$

49 is greater than 34.
34 is less than 49.

Visit ***The Learning Site*** **for additional ideas and activities.**
www.harcourtschool.com

ACTIVITY

Give your child three grocery items with prices of less than $1.00. Have your child line up the three items in order by price, from greatest to least and then from least to greatest.

Books to Share

To read about ordering numbers with your child, look for these books in your local library.

The Twelve Circus Rings,
by Seymour Chwast,
Harcourt, Brace & Company, 1996.

Seven Blind Mice,
by Ed Young,
Penguin Putnam, 1992.

Clams All Year,
by Maryann Cocca-Leffler,
Bantam Doubleday Dell, 1998.

Name ______________________

Ordinal Numbers

Write the correct position of each child.

1  sixth ______ 6th ______

2  ______ ______

3  ______ ______

4  ______ ______

5 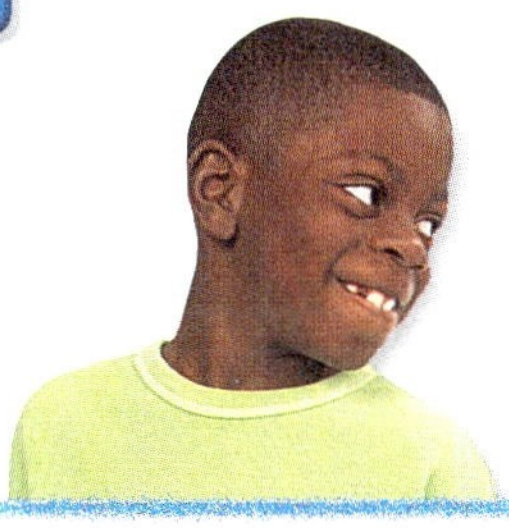 ______ ______

6 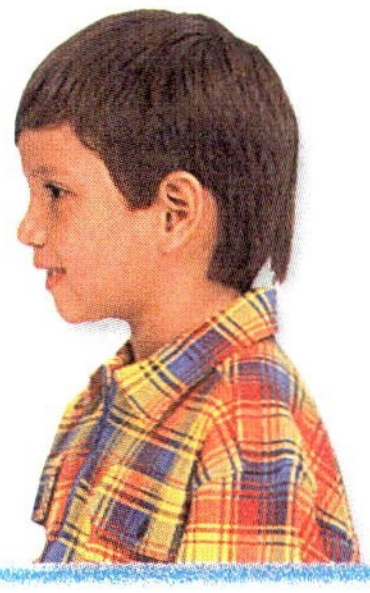 ______ ______

Talk About It ■ Reasoning

Does a line always begin at the left?

Practice

Color the floors.

- first RED
- 17th ORANGE
- 3rd BLUE
- sixth GREEN
- seventh PINK
- 15th YELLOW
- nineteenth BROWN
- 8th PURPLE
- 11th BLACK

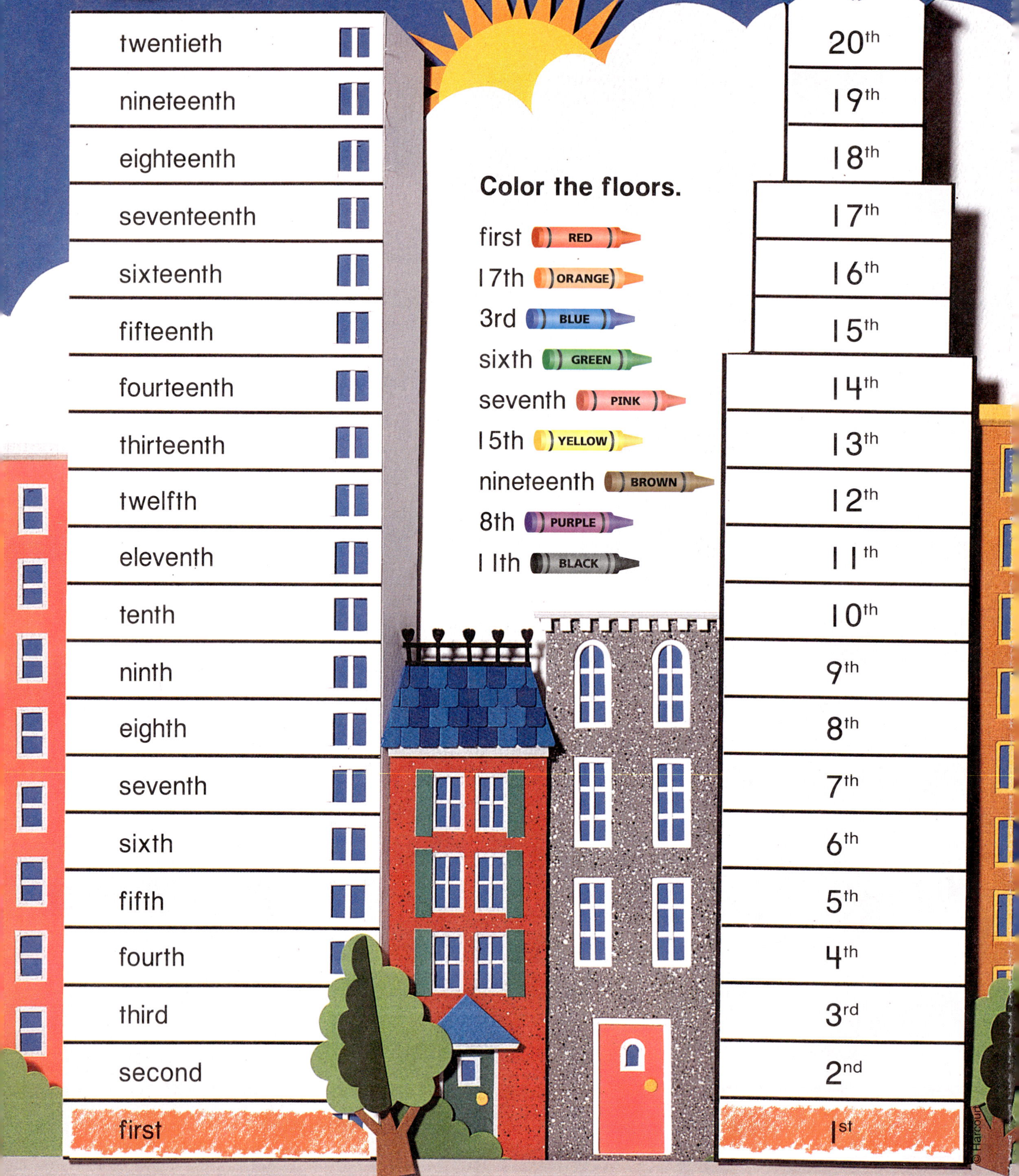

HOME ACTIVITY • Ask your child to identify the position of an object between 1st and 20th in a sequence.

Name ____________________

Compare Numbers: >, <, or =

Algebra

23 is greater than 13.

$23 > 13$

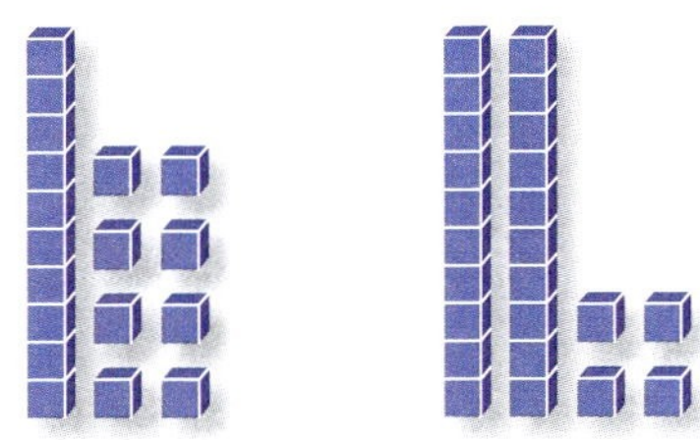

18 is less than 24.

$18 < 24$

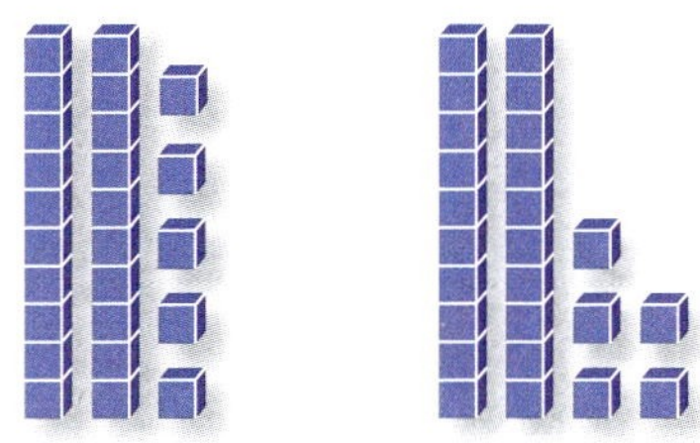

25 is equal to 25.

$25 = 25$

Write greater than, less than, or equal to. Then write >, <, or =.

1. 23 is less than 32.

   23 (<) 32

2. 40 is ______________ 41.

   40 ( ) 41

3. 54 is ______________ 45.

   54 ( ) 45

4. 19 is ______________ 19.

   19 ( ) 19

Talk About It ▪ **Reasoning**

How do you know that 35 is greater than 23?

Write greater than, less than, or equal to. Then write $>$, $<$, or $=$.

1. 98 is greater than 89.
   98 ($>$) 89

2. 5 is ______________ 15.
   5 ( ) 15

3. 35 is ______________ 38.
   35 ( ) 38

4. 60 is ______________ 59.
   60 ( ) 59

5. 27 is ______________ 27.
   27 ( ) 27

6. 76 is ______________ 67.
   76 ( ) 67

7. 56 is ______________ 36.
   56 ( ) 36

8. 31 is ______________ 31.
   31 ( ) 31

Problem Solving ■ Reasoning

Solve.
Show how you solved the problem.

9. Carlos is thinking of a number.
   It is between 20 and 40.
   It is 10 less than 40.
   What number is it? ______

HOME ACTIVITY • Have your child compare the prices of two grocery items that cost less than $1.00 each and tell which price is greater.

Name ______________________

Order Numbers: Before, After, Between

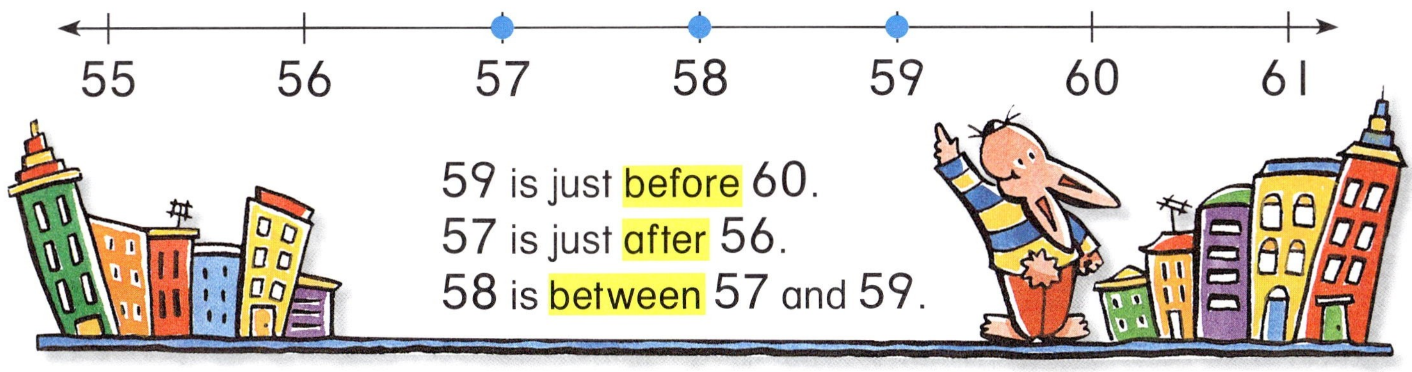

59 is just **before** 60.
57 is just **after** 56.
58 is **between** 57 and 59.

Write the number that is just before, just after, or between.

1. 26   27   28
2. ____   50   51
3. 35   ____   37
4. 89   ____   91
5. 14   ____   16
6. ____   31   32
7. 38   39   ____
8. 83   ____   85
9. ____   80   81
10. 8   9   ____
11. 17   18   ____
12. ____   44   45

Talk About It ■ Reasoning

How would you use before, after, and between to tell about these numbers?

Write the number that is just after, just before, or between.

	after	before	between
1	34, 35	39, 40	55, 56, 57
2	10, ____	____, 25	42, ____, 44
3	98, ____	____, 8	75, ____, 77
4	27, ____	____, 88	28, ____, 30
5	50, ____	____, 61	9, ____, 11
6	19, ____	____, 30	97, ____, 99
7	79, ____	____, 33	26, ____, 28
8	45, ____	____, 49	84, ____, 86

Mixed Review

9 Write the fact family for the set of numbers.

____ + ____ = ____   ____ + ____ = ____

____ − ____ = ____   ____ − ____ = ____

HOME ACTIVITY • Say a number. Have your child say the numbers that come just before and just after that number.

Name ______________________________

Even and Odd

Hands On

If each cube is in a pair, the number is **even**.
If one cube is left over, the number is **odd**.

1	2	3	4	5	6	7	8	9	10
odd	even	odd	even	odd	even	odd	even	odd	even

Show the number of cubes.
Snap the cubes together in pairs.
Write even or odd.

1. 12 even
2. 25 ______
3. 19 ______
4. 16 ______
5. 14 ______
6. 27 ______
7. 30 ______
8. 13 ______
9. 28 ______
10. 31 ______

Talk About It ▪ Reasoning

Look at the last digit of each number. How does it help you know whether the number is even or odd? Would a number ending in 0 be even or odd?

Show the number of cubes.
Write even or odd.

1 21 odd	**2** 24 ________
3 18 ________	**4** 22 ________
5 36 ________	**6** 29 ________
7 20 ________	**8** 23 ________
9 35 ________	**10** 27 ________
11 39 ________	**12** 34 ________
13 45 ________	**14** 40 ________
15 38 ________	**16** 41 ________

Problem Solving ■ Number Sense

17 How can you tell that a number that ends with 5, such as 85, is odd?

Use cubes to prove your answer.

HOME ACTIVITY • Give your child 20 small objects. Have him or her show you a number of objects between 1 and 20 and then tell you if the number is even or odd.

Name ____________________

Skip-Count

Count by twos. Write the numbers.

1

2, 4, 6, 8, 10, 12 flowers

Count by threes. Write the numbers.

2

3, ____, ____, ____, ____, ____ birds

Count by fours. Write the numbers.

3

4, ____, ____, ____, ____, ____ buses

Count by fives. Write the numbers.

4

5, ____, ____, ____, ____, ____ trees

Count by tens. Write the numbers.

5

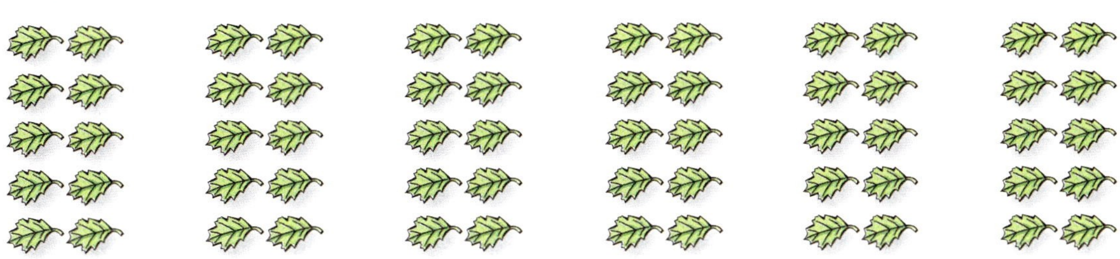

10, ____, ____, ____, ____, ____ leaves

Talk About It ■ Reasoning

What patterns do you see?

Practice

Count by twos. Color those boxes (yellow).
Count by threes. Draw a triangle around those numbers.
Count by fours. Color those boxes (green).
Count by fives. Color those boxes (orange).
Count by tens. Circle those numbers.

1

1	2	3	4	5	6	7	8	9	10
11	12	13	14	15	16	17	18	19	20
21	22	23	24	25	26	27	28	29	30
31	32	33	34	35	36	37	38	39	40
41	42	43	44	45	46	47	48	49	50
51	52	53	54	55	56	57	58	59	60
61	62	63	64	65	66	67	68	69	70
71	72	73	74	75	76	77	78	79	80
81	82	83	84	85	86	87	88	89	90
91	92	93	94	95	96	97	98	99	100

Problem Solving ▪ Number Sense

2 Count by fives.
Then count by tens.
Which numbers did you repeat?

HOME ACTIVITY • Ask your child to tell you what he or she notices about the numbers in the ones place when counting by tens.

Name ____________________

UNDERSTAND PLAN SOLVE CHECK

How many ears are on 5 horses?

UNDERSTAND What do you want to find out?

PLAN You can find a pattern to solve the problem.

Count by twos.

SOLVE

number of horses	1	2	3	4	5
number of ears	2	4	6		

There are 10 ears on 5 horses.

CHECK

Does your answer make sense? Explain.

1 How many wheels are on 6 cars?

number of cars	1	2	3	4	5	6
number of wheels	4	8				

There are _______ wheels on 6 cars.

2 How many pennies have the same value as 5 nickels?

number of nickels	1	2	3	4	5
number of pennies	5				

_______ pennies have the same value as 5 nickels.

What is the pattern rule? Find a pattern to complete the chart. Write how many.

1 How many wheels are on 7 tricycles?

number of tricycles	1	2	3	4	5	6	7
number of wheels	3	6	9				

There are _______ wheels on 7 tricycles.

2 How many legs are on 5 dogs?

number of dogs	1	2	3	4	5
number of legs	4				

There are _______ legs on 5 dogs.

Math Journal

Write About It

Suppose you are going to give each of your 6 friends 1 nickel. Complete a chart to show how many cents you will give away.

number of friends	1	2	3	4	5	6
number of cents	5¢					

HOME ACTIVITY • Ask your child to continue the patterns in the charts to tell how many ears are on 6 horses, how many wheels are on 7 cars, and so on.

Name ______________________________

CHECK ■ Concepts and Skills

Write greater than, less than, or equal to.
Then write >, <, or = in the circle.

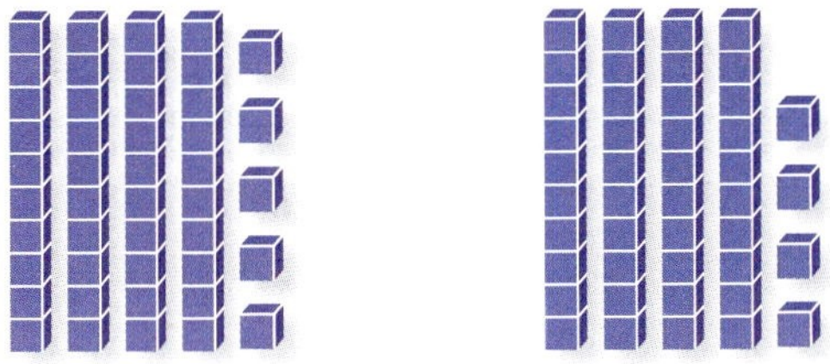

1 45 is ____________ than 44.

45 ◯ 44

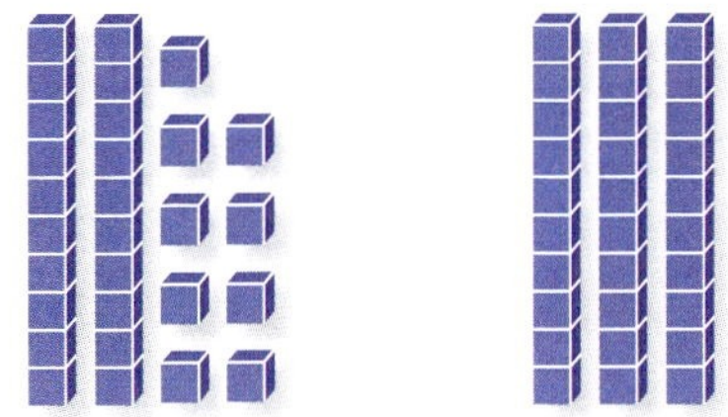

2 29 is ____________ than 30.

29 ◯ 30

Write the number that is just before, just after, or between.

3 ______, 20 69, ______ 86, ______, 88

Write even or odd.

4 35 ____________

Count by fours.

5 4, ____, ____, ____

CHECK ■ Problem Solving

What is the pattern rule? Find a pattern to complete the chart. Write how many.

6 How many legs are on 6 cats?

number of cats	1	2	3	4	5	6
number of legs	4	8				

There are ______ legs on 6 cats.

Name ______________________________

Choose the best answer for questions 1–4.

1 Which butterfly is fifth from the flower?

first

○ ○ ○ ○

2 What number is between 31 and 33?

29 ○ 30 ○ 32 ○ 34 ○

3 Which number is odd?

2 ○ 6 ○ 10 ○ 11 ○

4 How many legs are on 4 birds?

number of birds	1	2	3	4
number of legs	2			

2 ○ 4 ○ 8 ○ 10 ○

Show What You Know

5 Write each number in a box.
Then write >, <, or = in each circle.

23 76 50
91 44 84

CHAPTER 6

Data and Graphing

Make a graph to show the foods the animals are eating.

School Home Connection

Dear Family,
Today we started Chapter 6. We will learn how to make and use picture graphs, bar graphs, and pictographs. Here is the math vocabulary and an activity for us to do together at home.

Love,

____

My Math Words

bar graph
pictograph

Vocabulary

bar graph A graph that uses bars to stand for numbers

Toys Sold				
Tim				
Karen				
Rich				

0 1 2 3 4

pictograph A graph that uses pictures to stand for numbers

Toys Sold	
Tim	
Karen	
Rich	

Key: Each  stands for 2 toys.

Visit *The Learning Site* for additional ideas and activities. www.harcourtschool.com

Activity

Help your child make a graph to show how many cars, trucks, vans, and buses you see on a walk or a car ride to the store. Make a symbol on the graph for each one you see of each kind.

Books to Share

To read about graphs with your child, look for these books in your local library.

How Many Snails? A Counting Book, by Paul Giganti, Jr., William Morrow & Company, 1988.

Lemonade for Sale, by Stuart J. Murphy, HarperCollins, 1998.

Name ____________________

A **picture graph** is a way to show information. It uses pictures to stand for numbers.

Use the graph to answer the questions.

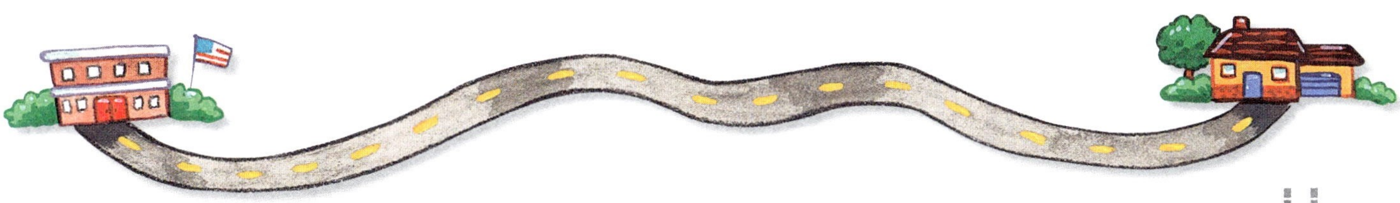

1. How many children come to school by car? 4

2. How many children walk to school? ______

3. How many more children come to school by bus than by car? ______

4. How many children in all walk or ride their bikes? ______

5. How many children in all come by bus or by car? ______

6. How many more children come to school by car than by bike? ______

Talk About It ■ Reasoning

Can you tell how many girls walk to school? Explain.

Use the graph to answer the questions.

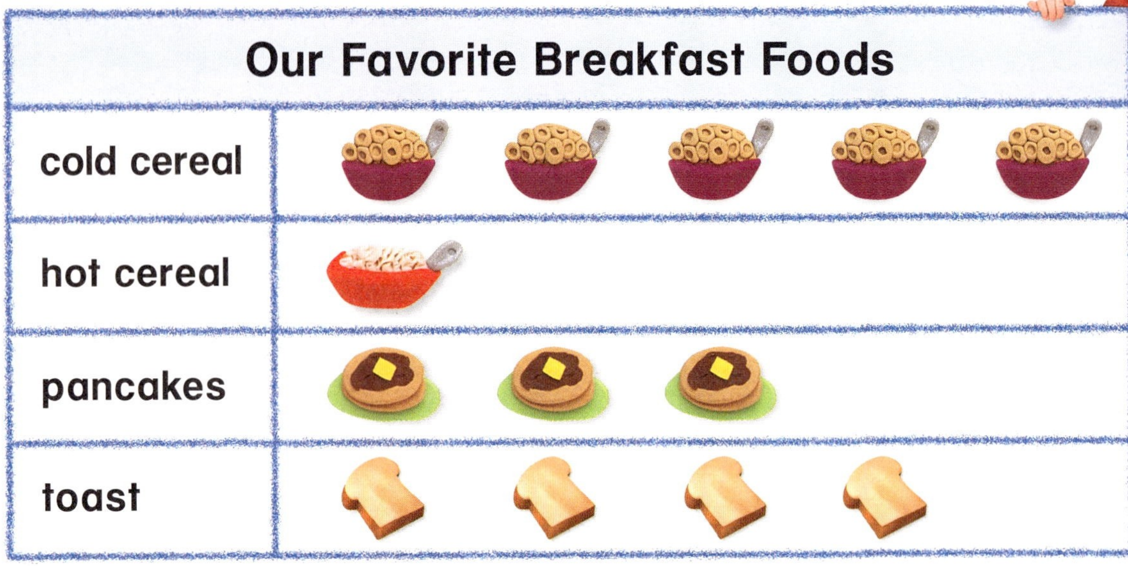

1. Which is the favorite breakfast food of the most people?

   cold cereal ______

2. Which is the favorite breakfast food of the fewest people?

   ______

3. How many more like pancakes than hot cereal? ______

4. How many fewer like hot cereal than cold cereal? ______

5. How many children in all were asked about their favorite breakfast food? ______

Problem Solving ■ Reasoning

6. How many more would have to choose hot cereal to make it the favorite of the most children? ______

HOME ACTIVITY • Have your child explain how he or she used each graph to answer the questions.

Name ______________________

Bar Graph

Use the graph to answer the questions.

A **bar graph** is a way to show information. It uses bars to show numbers.

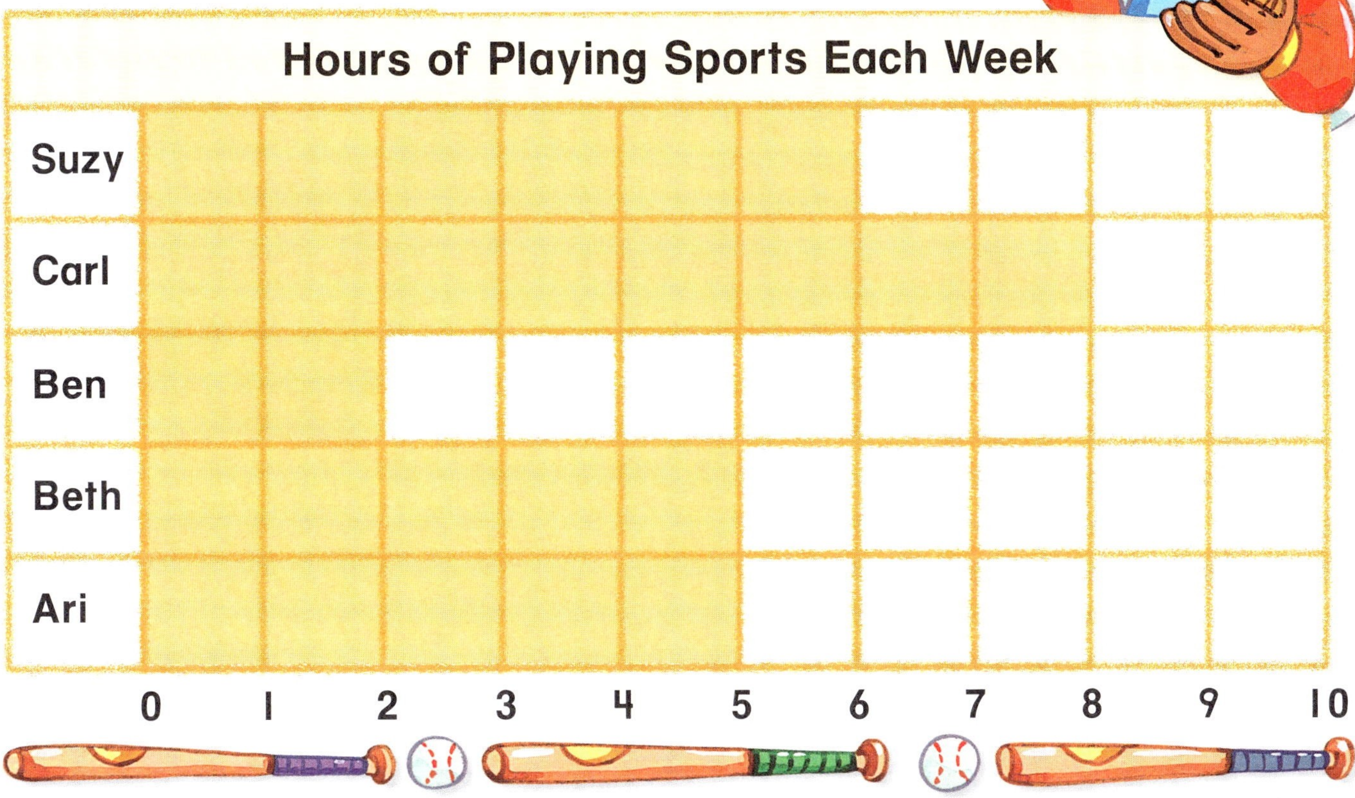

1. How many hours of sports does Ben play each week? 2

2. Which two children play sports for the same number of hours?

   ______________ and ______________

3. Who plays sports for the most hours? ________

4. What is the greatest number of hours spent playing sports? ________

5. What is the least number of hours spent playing sports? ________

Talk About It ▪ Reasoning

What does each colored box in the graph stand for?
What does each colored bar in the graph stand for?

Use the graph to answer the questions.

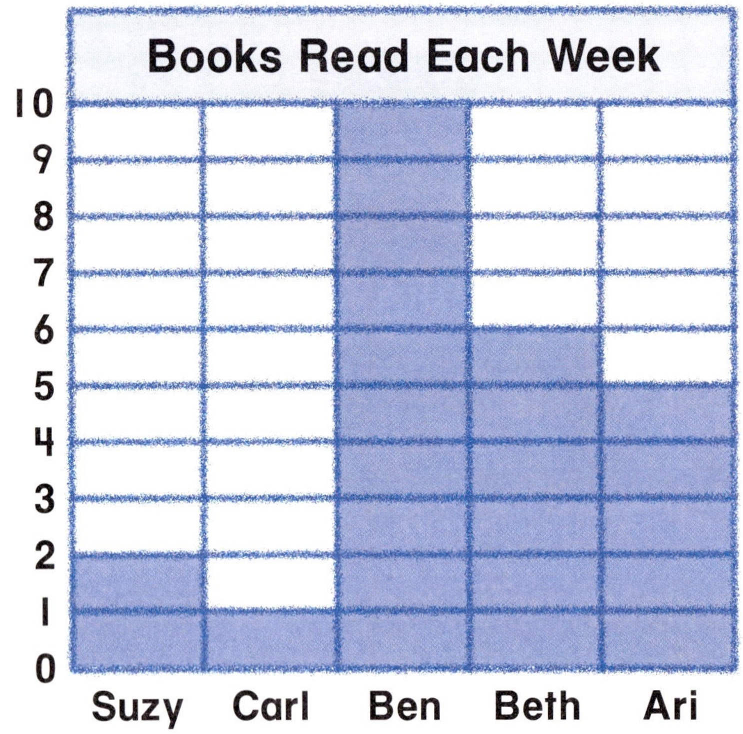

1. How many books does Ben read each week? 10

2. How many books do Suzy and Carl read altogether? ______

3. Who reads the fewest books? ____________

4. How many more books does Ben read than Ari? ______

Problem Solving ▪ Reasoning

5. Look at the book graph. Can you tell how many fiction books Ben read? Explain your thinking.

____

HOME ACTIVITY • Have your child explain how he or she used each graph to answer the questions.

Name ______________________________

UNDERSTAND › PLAN › SOLVE › CHECK

Arthur wanted to find out which sandwiches his classmates liked best. He asked each child and made a **tally table** to show their answers.

Then he made a graph with the same information.

Our Favorite Sandwiches	
cheese	III
bologna	~~IIII~~ II
hamburger	~~IIII~~ I
tuna	III

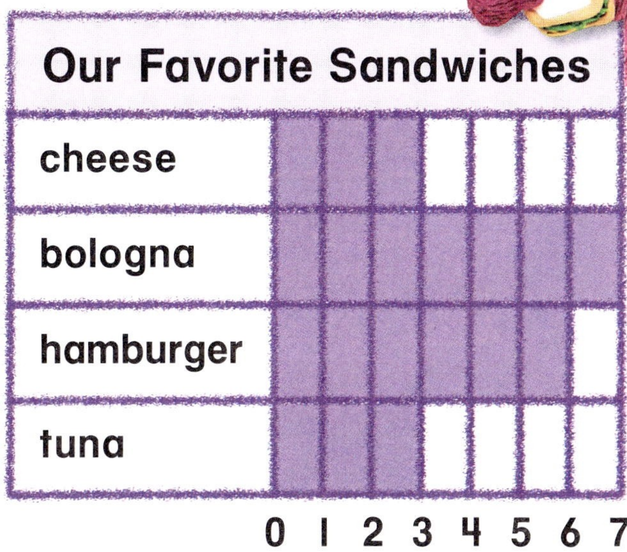

Use the graph to answer the questions.

1. Which sandwich is the favorite of the most people? bologna

2. Which two sandwiches are the favorites of the same number of people?

______________________ and ______________________

3. How many more like bologna than hamburger? ____ − ____ = ____

4. How many in all like cheese or hamburger? ____ + ____ = ____

5. How many in all like bologna or tuna? ____ + ____ = ____

6. How many more like hamburger than tuna? ____ − ____ = ____

Our Favorite Colors	
blue	卌 I
red	I
green	II
yellow	III

Use the graph to answer the questions.

1. What is the favorite color of the most children? blue
2. What is the favorite color of the fewest children? ______
3. How many more children like yellow than red? ____ − ____ = ____
4. How many children in all like blue or green? ____ + ____ = ____
5. How many in all like blue or yellow? ____ + ____ = ____
6. How many more like blue than yellow? ____ − ____ = ____
7. How many more like blue than red? ____ − ____ = ____

Math Journal

Write About It

Write a question about the graph.
Ask a friend to answer it.

HOME ACTIVITY • Have your child explain how he or she used each graph to answer the questions.

Name ______________________________

Take a Survey

Which season do your classmates like best?
Take a survey and make a graph to find out.

1. Ask ten people which season is their favorite. Fill in the tally table to show their answers.
2. Use the tally table to fill in the graph.

Our Favorite Seasons	
winter	
spring	
summer	
fall	

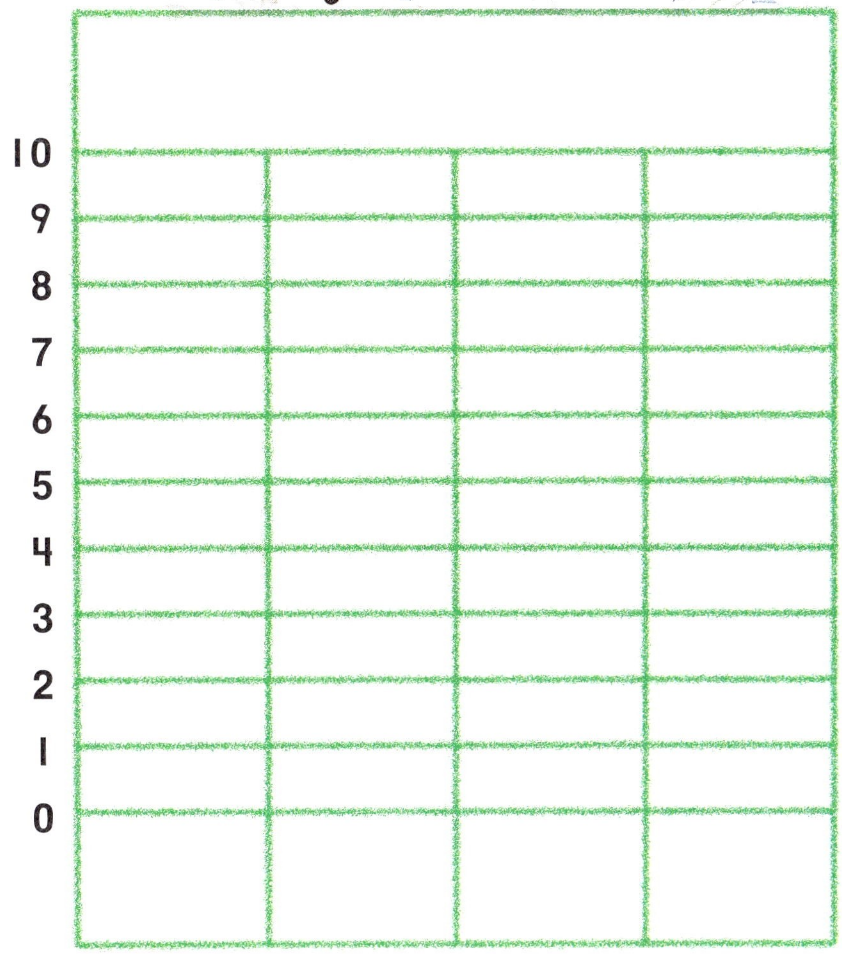

3. Which season do the most people in your class like best?

____

4. Do more people in your class like winter or summer best?

____

5. Do more people in your class like fall or spring best?

____

Talk About It ■ Reasoning

What addition and subtraction questions can you make up about the graph?

Which day of the week do your classmates like best? Take a survey and make a graph to find out.

1. Ask ten people which day of the week is their favorite. Fill in the tally table to show their answers.

2. Use the tally table to fill in the graph.

Our Favorite Days of the Week	
Sunday	
Monday	
Tuesday	
Wednesday	
Thursday	
Friday	
Saturday	

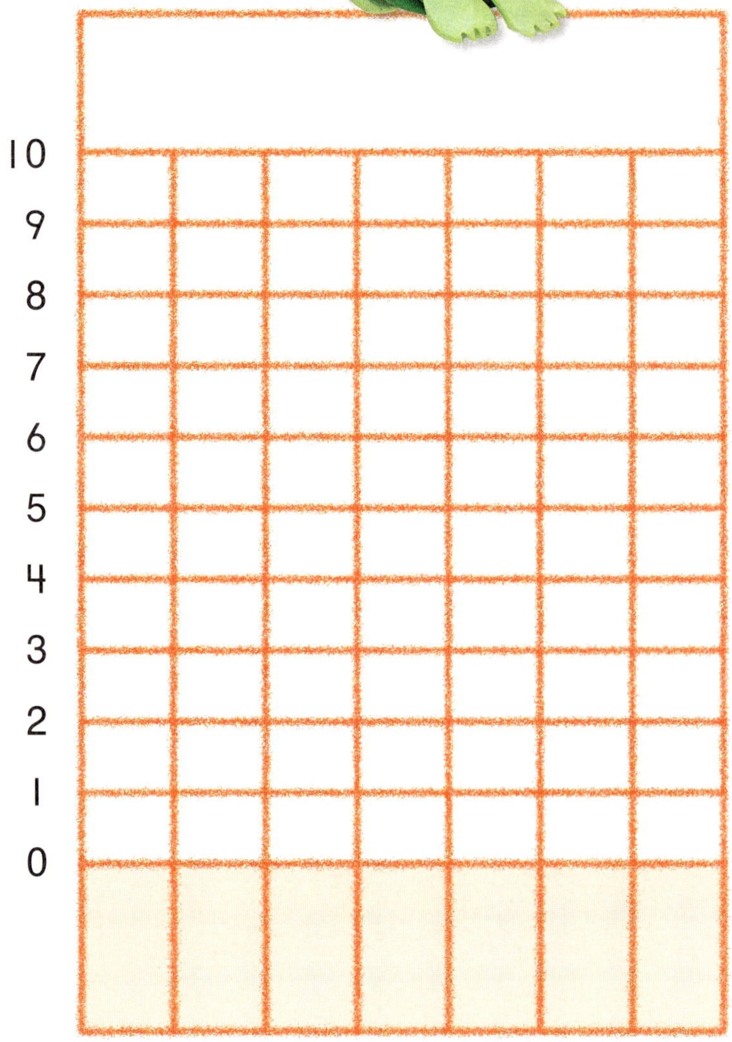

3. Which day do the most people in your class like best? ____________________

4. Do more people in your class like Saturday or Sunday best? ____________________

5. Do more people in your class like Monday or Friday best? ____________________

6. Which day do the fewest people like best? ____________________

HOME ACTIVITY • **Have your child survey family members about their favorite snacks and then show on a graph what he or she learns.**

Name ______________________________

Use the table to fill in the bar graph.

Books Sold	
Kate	10
Chen	8
John	18
Jenny	2
Cory	8

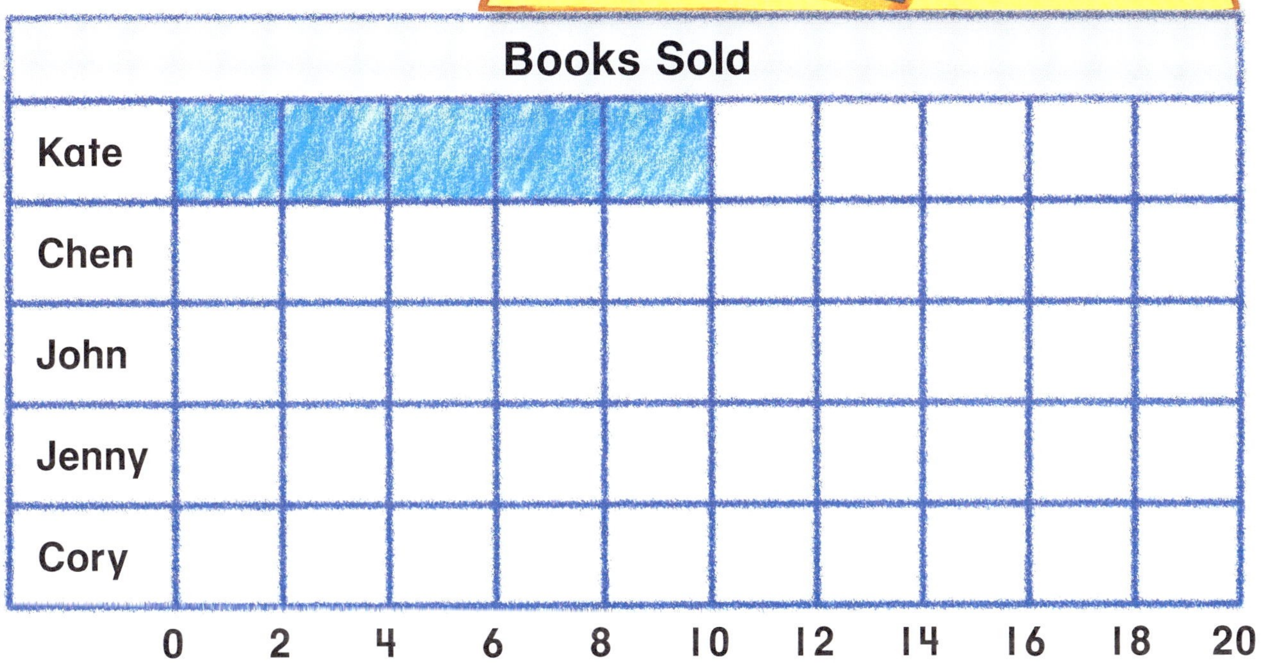

Key: Each ☐ stands for 2 books sold.

1. What is the greatest number of books sold? ______

2. What is the least number of books sold? ______

3. What is the difference between the greatest number of books sold and the least? ______

Talk About It ▪ Reasoning

Which three children together sold the same number of books as John?

Use the table to fill in the bar graph.

Number of Children in Second Grade at Bell School	
Class 2A	20
Class 2B	18
Class 2C	18
Class 2D	16

Number of Children in Second Grade at Bell School

Class 2A										
Class 2B										
Class 2C										
Class 2D										
	0	2	4	6	8	10	12	14	16	18	20

Key: Each ☐ stands for 2 children.

1. How many children are in the largest class? ______
2. How many children are in the smallest class? ______
3. What is the difference between the numbers of children in the largest and smallest classes? ______

Problem Solving ■ Application

4. Think of a question you can ask your classmates. Show their answers in a table or graph. Explain your table or graph.

HOME ACTIVITY • Have your child ask family members about their favorite things to do and then make a graph to show what he or she learns.

Use Pictographs

Children Who Walk to School	
Tosha's Class	卌 卌 卌
Linda's Class	卌 卌
Carolyn's Class	卌 卌 卌 卌 卌
Barb's Class	卌 卌 卌 卌

A **pictograph** uses pictures to show how many.

Use the tally table to fill in the pictograph.
Draw 1  for every 5 children.

Children Who Walk to School	
Tosha's Class	
Linda's Class	
Carolyn's Class	
Barb's Class	

Key: Each  stands for 5 children.

1. How many walkers are there in Tosha's class? 15

2. How many children in Tosha's class and Linda's class walk to school? ______

3. Which class has the most walkers? ______________

4. Write a question to ask about the graph.

____

____

Talk About It ■ Reasoning

Why do the symbols on graphs sometimes stand for more than one object?

Classmates Who Have Pets	
birds	IIII
cats	𝍸 III
dogs	𝍸 𝍸 IIII
fish	𝍸 I

Use the tally table to fill in the pictograph.
Draw 1 🧍 for every 2 children.

Classmates Who Have Pets	
birds	🧍 🧍
cats	
dogs	
fish	

Key: Each 🧍 stands for 2 children.

1. How many more children have dogs than cats? ______

2. Which kind of pet do the fewest children have? ______________

3. Write a question to ask about the graph.

____

____

HOME ACTIVITY • Ask your child to imagine that each picture in the graph on this page stands for 10 children. Have him or her answer question 1 again.

Name ______________________

CHECK ■ Concepts and Skills

Use the pictograph to answer the questions.

Key: Each (figure) stands for 5 children.

1. How many people like reading best? ______

2. How many people like math best? ______

3. How many more children like math than science? ______

CHECK ■ Problem Solving

Use the tally table to fill in the bar graph.

Our Favorite Sports	
basketball	||||
football	|||
baseball	|
soccer	||||

Our Favorite Sports				
basketball				
football				
baseball				
soccer				
	0 1	2	3	4

Use the graph to answer the questions.

4. How many more children like soccer than baseball? ______

5. How many children in all like football or basketball? ______

Name ______________________________

Choose the best answer for questions 1–3.

1 The graph shows favorite animals.
How many children in all chose dogs or birds?

3 ○ 7 ○ 8 ○ 11 ○

2 Skip count. Which number is missing?

3, 6, 9, ___, 15, 18

21 ○ 14 ○ 12 ○ 11 ○

3 What is the sum?

$2 + 3 + 8 =$ ___

5 ○ 10 ○ 11 ○ 13 ○

Show What You Know

4 Use red, green, and yellow. Color the apples.

Fill in the tally table. Fill in the bar graph.

Color of Apples		
Color	**Tally**	**Total**
Red		
Green		
Yellow		

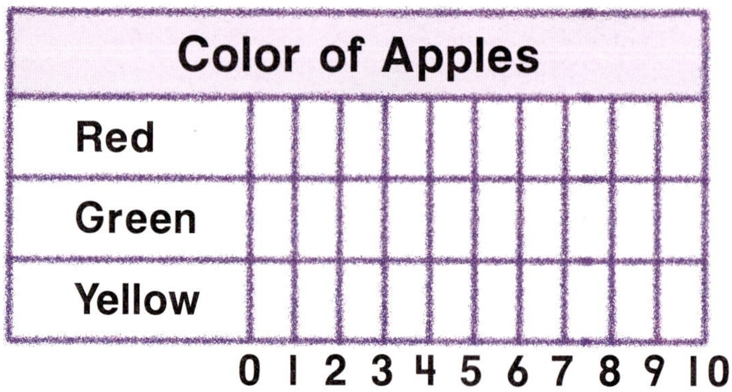

Get on the Bus

written by Ann Lee
illustrated by Annie Lunsford

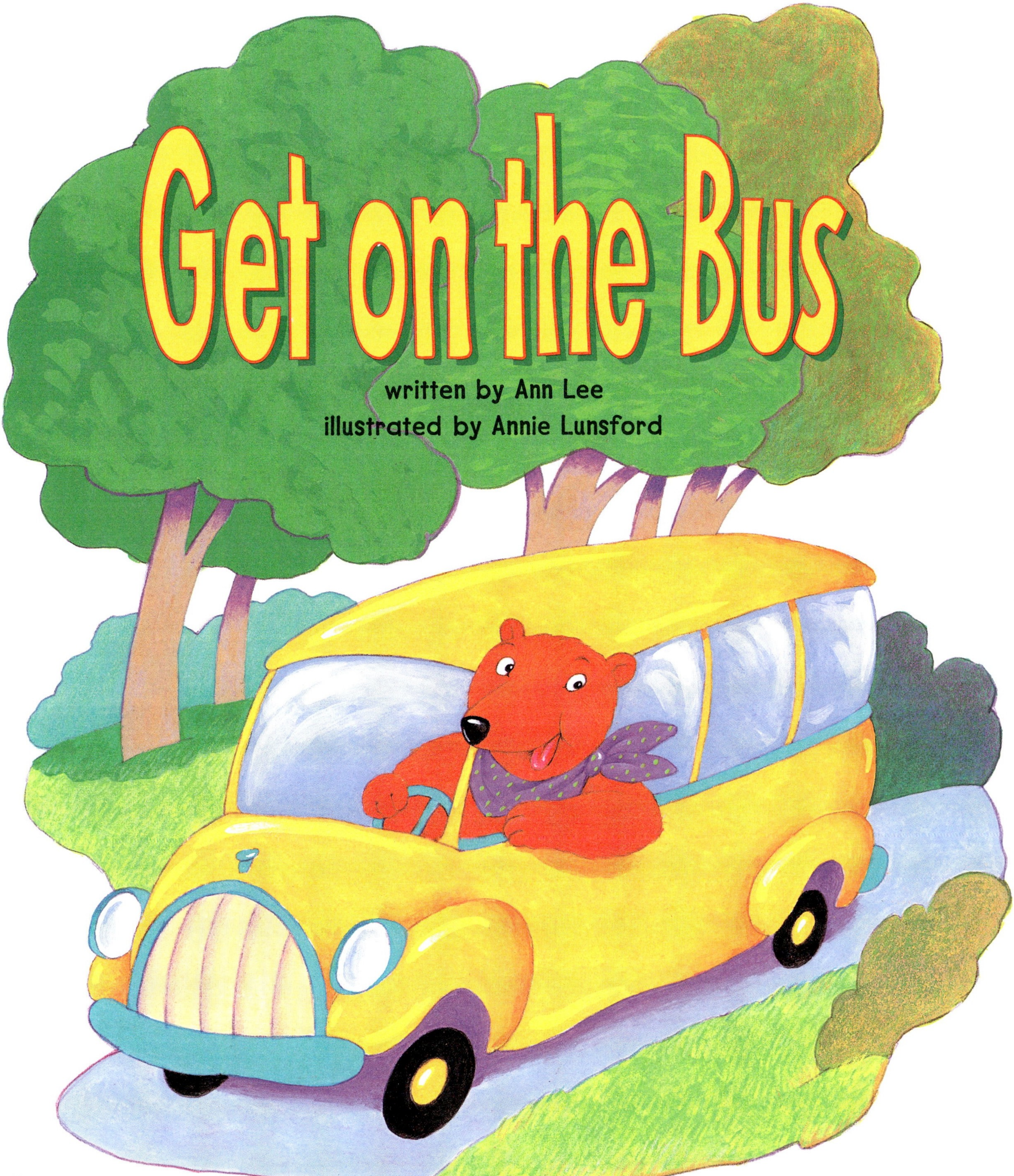

This book will help me review counting by tens.

This book belongs to ____________________.

Bear got into his big yellow bus to take some animals to their yearly picnic. "My bus holds only 100 animals," he said.

Bear came to the pond and saw some frogs. "Are there 100 of you?" he asked the frogs.

"No," said one frog. "There are _______ of us." The frogs got into Bear's big yellow bus.

The frogs were singing in the bus as Bear drove on down the road. A swarm of bees flew around the bus. "Are there 100 of you?" Bear asked the bees.

"No," said one bee. "There are ______ of us." The bees flew into the bus and sang with the frogs.

Pretty soon a big bunch of grasshoppers came jumping along. "Are there 100 of you?" asked Bear. The animals in the bus stopped singing to listen to Bear and the grasshoppers.

"No," said one grasshopper. "There are _______ of us." The grasshoppers got on top of the bus.

Bear drove the bus until he came to some songbirds sitting on tree branches. "Hi!" said Bear. "Are there 100 of you?"

"No," said one bird. "There are _______ of us." The songbirds flew to the top of the bus and joined the grasshoppers.

Bear and the animals arrived at the picnic place. The frogs, the bees, the grasshoppers, and the songbirds were excited to be together at the picnic. As Bear drove away, he heard one bee say, "Now there are 100 of us!"

Name ____________________________

Problem Solving
Math Detective

Crack the Codes

Use your skills to find the answers to these riddles. First, solve each problem. Then match each number to the letter. Good luck!

a	b	c	d	e	f	g	h	i	j	k	l	m
1	2	3	4	5	6	7	8	9	10	11	12	13
n	**o**	**p**	**q**	**r**	**s**	**t**	**u**	**v**	**w**	**x**	**y**	**z**
14	15	16	17	18	19	20	21	22	23	24	25	26

What type of ship never sinks?

$9 - 3$	$9 + 9$	$5 + 4$	$0 + 5$	$16 - 2$	$3 + 1$	$10 + 9$	$12 - 4$	$6 + 3$	$8 + 8$

What sings and flies but doesn't swim?

$10 - 9$		$4 + 4$	$26 - 5$	$6 + 7$	$15 - 2$	$8 + 1$	$10 + 4$	$3 + 4$	$10 - 8$	$8 + 1$	$11 + 7$	$13 - 9$

Stretch Your Thinking Make up a riddle in code for your classmates to solve.

Name ______________________________

Challenge
$<$, $>$, or $=$

$4 + 2 \;(>)\; 5$

$4 + 2 = 6$

6 is greater than 5

Write $<$, $>$, or $=$ to complete the number sentence.

1	$5 + 1 \bigcirc 6$	2	$10 + 2 \bigcirc 13$
3	$8 - 3 \bigcirc 2$	4	$7 - 3 \bigcirc 4$
5	$6 + 3 \bigcirc 5 + 3$	6	$4 + 2 \bigcirc 1 + 5$
7	$10 - 7 \bigcirc 14 - 11$	8	$9 - 3 \bigcirc 4 - 2$
9	$1 + 15 \bigcirc 17 - 1$	10	$8 + 3 \bigcirc 7 + 5$
11	$14 - 7 \bigcirc 15 - 7$	12	$18 + 3 \bigcirc 24 - 3$

Name ______________________________

Skills and Concepts

Add or subtract.

1 10 + 0 = ____

0 + 10 = ____

2 9 + 9 = ____

9 + 10 = ____

3 9 + ____ = 16

4 4 + 5 + 1 = ____

5 13 − 13 = ____

6 12 − 2 = ____

7 Write the fact family for the set of numbers.

6, 7, 13

____ + ____ = ____ ____ − ____ = ____

____ + ____ = ____ ____ − ____ = ____

8 Write how many tens and ones in three different ways.

____ tens ____ ones = ____

____ + ____ = ____

____

9 Circle the value of the underlined digit.

$\underline{8}2$

8 or 80

10 Read the number. Write the number in different ways.

sixty-two

______ tens + ______ ones

______ + ______

______

11 Write the correct position of the bee.

first

______

12 Write greater than, less than, or equal to.

28 is _________ 30

28 ◯ 30

13 Show the number of cubes. Write odd or even.

____

14 Use the tally table. How many children chose oranges?

______ children

Our Favorite Fruits	
apple	II
bananas	IIII
oranges	~~IIII~~ II

Each I stands for 1 child's vote.

Problem Solving

15 Use the graph. How many children in all like apples or bananas?

______ children

Name ______________________________

Veggie Soup

Paul wants to use at least one of each type of vegetable to make his soup.

Write how many of each vegetable Paul can use if he chooses 15 vegetables.

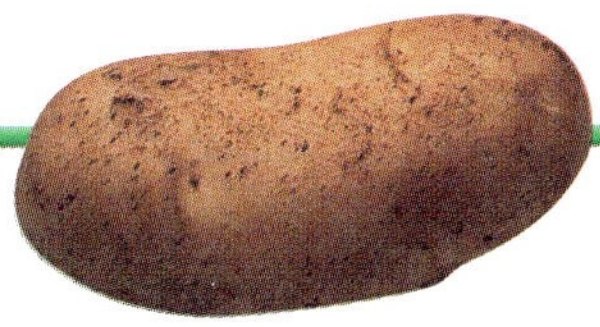 ________  ________  ________  ________

Show your work.

Tech

Name ______________________________

The Learning Site • Addition Surprise

1. Go to **www.harcourtschool.com.**
2. Click on  .
3. Drag the sums into the table.
4. What picture did you find?

Practice and Problem Solving

Write the missing number.

1. $5 + 3 =$ ____

2. $3 + 7 =$ ____

3. ____ $+ 9 = 18$

4. $4 +$ ____ $= 12$

5. First there were 6 birds.
Then ____ birds came.
Now there are 15 birds.

6. First, there were ____ birds.
Then 4 birds came.
Now there are 12 birds.

Name ______________________________

PROBLEM SOLVING ON LOCATION

In Our Nation's Capital

Washington, D.C., is the capital of our country. Tourists like to visit many interesting places there.

Which of these places would you and your classmates most like to visit?

Capitol Building

Washington Monument

National Air and Space Museum

White House

Fill in the tally table to show the votes. Use the tally table to fill in the graph.

Places We Would Like to Visit		
	Tally	**Total**
White House		
Capitol Building		
Washington Monument		
National Air and Space Museum		

Places We Would Like to Visit												
White House												
Capitol Building												
Washington Monument												
National Air and Space Museum												
	0 2	4	6	8	10	12	14	16	18	20	22	24

Name ______________________________

PROBLEM SOLVING ON LOCATION

In the Forest

Many kinds of animals live in South Carolina. Here are just a few you might see in the state parks and forests there.

deer

robin

beaver

turkey

dragonfly

black bear

bee

Sort these animals.
Write each name where you think it belongs.

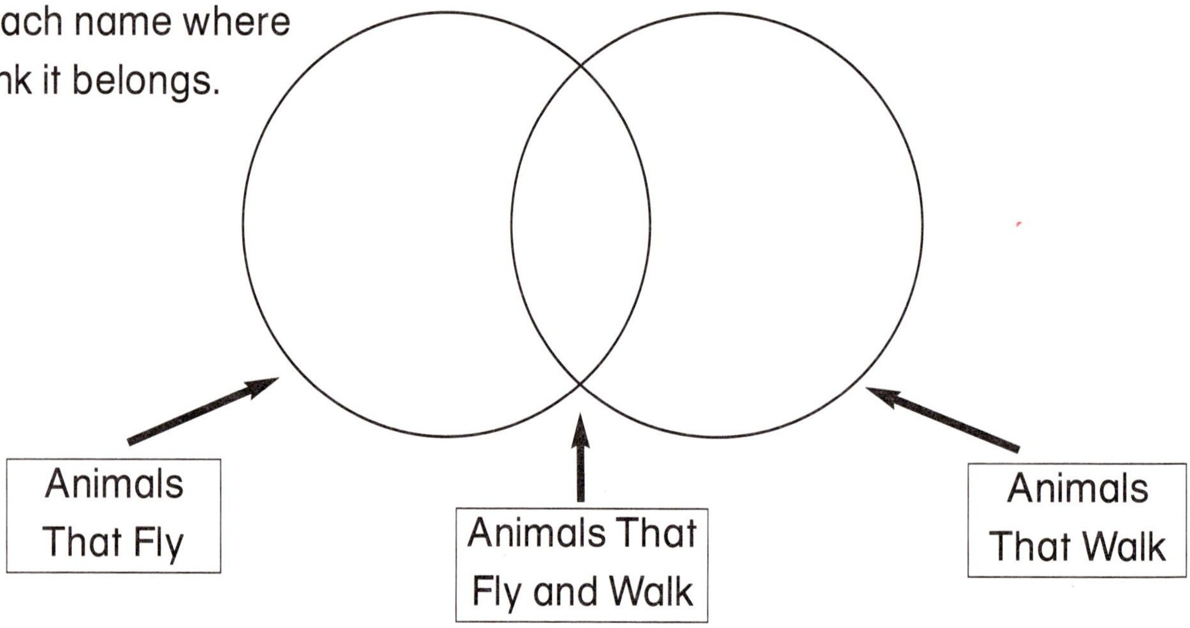